WOMEN'S SOCCER

Using Science to Improve Speed

Dr. Michael Yessis

Wish Publishing
Terre Haute, Indiana
www.wishpublishing.com

Cover designed by Phil Velikan
Cover photography by arrangement with Corbis www.corbis.com
Interior photography by Dr. Michael Yessis
Proofread by Ken Samelson

Printed in the United States of America
10 9 8 7 6 5 4 3 2

Published in the United States by
Wish Publishing
P.O. Box 10337
Terre Haute, IN 47801, USA
www.wishpublishing.com

Distributed in the United States by
Cardinal Publishers Group
7301 Georgetown Road, Suite 118
Indianapolis, Indiana 46268

This book is dedicated to all female soccer players regardless of age or level of playing ability. I hope it gives you the ability to run and cut well (the keys to better playing), so that you can play to your best potential and get the greatest enjoyment possible from this terrific sport.

Acknowledgements

I am deeply indebted to many people who have helped make this book possible. They were very gracious with their time and effort to provide the book with many of its unique features. Each person played a very important role, thus, the order in which their names appear is not related to the value of their contribution. More specifically, I would like to thank:

Sasha Araya-Schrarer, who not only served as a model for some of the running and cutting actions, but also for many of the strength and flexibility exercises. She is a member of the San Diego Surf Soccer Club.

Maile Tavepholjalern, for serving as a model for the running and cutting actions as well as being a demonstrator of many of the jump and strength exercises. She is a member of the San Diego Surf Soccer Club.

Kirsten Rogers, for serving as a model for the running and cutting actions. She is a member of the National Champion Under-17 San Diego Surf Soccer Club team.

Megan Kakadelas, for serving as a model for many of the running and cutting actions. She is a member of the National Champion Under-17 San Diego Surf Soccer Club team.

Sarah Davis, who served as a model for the running and cutting actions. She is a member of the San Diego Surf Soccer Club.

Natasha Dziamidzenka, for serving as a model for some of the strength and explosive exercises.

Alison Spencer for serving as a model for the running and cutting actions. She is a member of the San Diego Surf Soccer Club.

Marissa Yessis, my daughter and former soccer player, who filled in as a model for some key cutting actions, strength and explosive exercises. In addition she inputted all the pictures seen in this book into the computer for processing.

Nancy Kauler, for serving as a model for the running actions. She is a member of the Rip Tyed team in the Adult Woman's Arena Soccer league.

Jerre Walker, for serving as a model for the running actions. She is a member of the Rip Tyed team in the Adult Woman's Soccer league.

A.S. Rogers for his help in getting permission to use the Surf team girls for this book.

Teresa Kakadelas, Team Manager for the San Diego Surf Soccer Club, who was very helpful in getting the girls who were interested in being a part of this book. Also for contacting and following up with the girls when needed.

Edie Yessis, my lovely wife, who not only allowed me to bounce ideas off her, but for her patience and understanding during the course of working on this book.

Table of Contents

Chapter One
Speed and Quickness can be Improved   1

Chapter Two
**The Role of Specialized Strength
and Explosive Exercises**   9

Chapter Three
Analysis of Running Technique   17

Chapter Four
Agility: Analysis of Cutting Actions   47

Chapter Five
**Specialized Strength Exercises
for Running and Cutting**   71

Chapter Six
Specialized Explosive Exercises   105

Chapter Seven
Active Stretches   133

Chapter Eight
**Common Running and Cutting Errors
and their Corrections**   147

Chapter Nine
Nutrition for Optimal Playing   *161*

Chapter Ten
Designing Your Exercise Program   *181*

Chapter Eleven
Women's Issues   *207*

Speed and Quickness Can Be Improved

Playing soccer is easy. All you have to do is run and kick the ball into a net — if you are a serious player, you will be laughing at this comment. Women's soccer has evolved into a very complex and physically demanding sport. Not only must you be able to kick and pass the ball well, but you must be able to get into position to execute the most favorable shot and keep up with or away from your opponent. For this you must be fast and quick and be able to change directions while in motion to get away from your opponent on offense and to keep up with your opponent on defense.

The trend in modern soccer is toward improved and greater players' abilities and functions. This in turn leads to execution of a greater number of sprints or dashes at high intensity, i.e., maximum speed. It is not uncommon to find that the total dash or sprint distance run at top speeds exceeds 2,000 yards. And the number of such dashes is well over one hundred. On some teams, because of the constant use of supercharged speed tactics, the number of fast changes in play require an even greater number of quick dashes and changes in direction.

The energy for this speed and quickness work comes from the anaerobic pathways, i.e., the work is executed without the benefit of oxygen for production of energy. In other words, your breathing, in which you get oxygen for energy, is not capable of supplying the energy needed for these quick all-out, high-intensity dashes. In addition, even a 3-second all-out run leads to significant depletion of your energy stores, especially ATP and creatine phosphate. Because of this, soccer requires a greater ability to develop short lasting, maximum efforts more than the ability to maintain effort over a long period of time. The higher your level of play, the greater is the need for executing short lasting, maximum effort.

Goalkeepers are usually superior in both their anaerobic power and energy expenditure. This position involves explosive efforts in kicks, throws, etc., and as a result, they must spend considerable time training for speed-strength (power). In other words, their game functions require a combination of strength and speed and the ability to demonstrate explosive movements generated very quickly. Backs and forwards have nearly identical anaerobic capabilities whereas, halfbacks lag somewhat behind, since they require a higher endurance level than other positions mainly because they are in almost constant motion during the game. Because of this, the energy capabilities of halfbacks are skewed more toward aerobic capacity rather than anaerobic as required in most of the other positions.

To play well requires not only good playing strategy and the ability to execute various plays and shots but you must have the physical ability to run fast and to make quick cuts in order to carry out your functions. To improve their abilities, most players spend more time playing, buy different equipment and seek out a better coach or team. These methods work in some instances but they will never allow you to achieve your full potential. If you are a gifted player and have the ability to run, cut quickly and execute the skills and strategies required, you can probably become a good player fairly quickly. But you should understand that only about one out of every one hundred thousand players is truly gifted.

For most of you who cannot exhibit these skills "naturally," there are very effective ways available to perfect your soccer play so that you can be on a par with, if not better than, the more gifted player. Regardless of the recommendations given to you by a coach, you must have the physical ability to run well, cut as quickly as possible and to kick and pass accurately. In addition to the skills, you need adequate strength and flexibility to execute well, the actions involved in the different skills. If you do not, you are doomed to failure regardless of how much money you spend, clinics you attend and practice you put in. Your playing ability can only be as good as your physical abilities allow.

Most important to understand is that you *can* improve your skills especially your ability to run faster and make quicker cuts (changes in direction while running). You do this by perfecting your running and cutting technique and developing your physical abilities as they relate to execution of these skills. When you develop your physical abilities in the same basic movement patterns seen in execution of these skills, you can attain your true genetic potential. Each of you can do this and in a relatively short period of time.

Doing specialized exercises to improve your speed, strength, flexibility, speed of movement, reaction time and technique will improve your playing ability beyond your wildest expectations. This book will show you how to do this through *The Yessis System of Improving Performance*. It is a system that has been developed after working with thousands of athletes who significantly improved their speed and quickness by making changes in their technique and improving their physical abilities specific to the skills involved. By doing exercises specific to running and cutting, you will also be improving your jumping and kicking ability since many of the muscle and joint actions involved are the same. As a result, you will achieve multiple goals with minimal work.

By improving technique and increasing strength, flexibility and explosiveness specific to running and cutting, you will find it easier to execute game strategy with less effort and more confidence. You will find that you have greater control and feel for skill execution especially in regard to speed and quickness. When specialized physical training to increase strength and flexibility is coupled with speed and explosive training, the results are even more impressive.

It is generally understood among soccer players that weight (strength) training can lead to greater speed, power and overall game play. In some quarters, however, the need for strength training has not been universally accepted. In fact, many players and coaches still believe that weight training will make them slower, decrease their flexibility, and lead to injury. Others believe that only boys should weight train and that weight training for girls is dangerous. These are myths that have persisted in soccer (and other sports) for many years and should be dispelled. Weight training, when done correctly, is a female soccer player's ally.

Depending upon the type of weight training program that you undertake, you can: (1) improve kicking power, (2) increase running speed and quickness, (3) increase muscular and aerobic endurance, (4) lessen the chances of injury, and (5) increase jump height. By tailoring the weight training program to fit your needs, you can develop any specific type of strength that is needed. This includes strength-endurance, absolute strength, speed-strength, eccentric strength, explosive strength, and starting strength. You should not think of strength training simply as a means of getting bigger or stronger. Think of it as a means of improving specific aspects of your game.

Reading this book may be the first step on your pathway to getting the fullest possible enjoyment and satisfaction from playing soccer. By carrying out the recommendations given in this book you will be amazed at how much progress you can make in a relatively short time. This applies not only to making changes in your running and cutting technique but also in regard to specific physical problems that you may have.

For example, many players are plagued by hamstring or lower back problems. But these are some the easiest to take care of! Although this may seem hard to believe, it has been proven time and time again not only with soccer players but with athletes in other sports as well. In this book you will see how this is done, so that you too can play pain-free.

Although soccer is a team sport it is also very individualized according to playing position and your mental and physical abilities. However, regardless of how you run and cut, there are specific actions that everyone must be able to do in order to play most successfully. How well you execute these actions depends on your physical abilities. More specifically, your physical abilities determine: (1) how much you rely on each joint action, (2) the range of motion of each action, and (3) the force involved in each joint action.

You can find many general descriptions of what occurs in running and cutting but not an analysis. For example, I heard a top running coach talk about improving running speed to soccer coaches. He spent a considerable amount of time talking about how the body should be held, how the arms and legs must be moved quickly, how the elbow should remain bent, how the landing should be soft and other general factors. After a long discourse on running posture, he went directly to talking about some of the girls that he had coached and their successes. At no time in his talk did he bring out what actions occurred in sprinting or how they could be improved. In essence, he talked about running but not the how-to of running.

An analysis, especially an applied biomechanical analysis, is quite different. It answers such questions as: is the running or cutting effective? If so, why is it effective? What is the role of each joint action? Which joint actions can be changed to make the technique more effective? How can the specific actions be made more powerful? Should the running or cutting technique be modified? If so, how? Most standard instruction does not address these points. Instead, you may read articles and books and look at videos related to the opinions of coaches and players which are often at odds with one another.

For example, in running, you have probably read or been told that the heel of the foot should make first contact on the ground. But from biomechanics we know that the heel hit can cause injury and slow you down because of the braking forces produced. The forces generated when the heel hits the ground, which momentarily stop your lower body movement, can be extremely high and are usually the culprit in many leg and foot injuries. Equally important is that the heel hit does not utilize the economical and speed functions of the foot and leg tendons and muscles. Thus, by applying some of the laws of biomechanics, it is possible to come up with accurate descriptions of what takes place in running and cutting and the role each key joint action plays. This is one of the key features included in this book. (See the many cinematograms of different players in Chapters 3 and 4.)

Improving your physical abilities plays an important role in developing effective running technique and increasing running speed and quickness. The more you can improve your physical abilities to run faster and cut quicker, the more effective your playing will be. Keep in mind that regardless of your position or value on the team, you must still be able to carry out your assignments and to "come through" when the odds are against you.

I have biomechanically analyzed many of the best soccer players (and sprinters) in the world to determine the key joint actions that they execute in running and cutting and to evaluate their effectiveness. To be as objective as possible, the key joint actions in running and cutting and when they occur were identified through high speed videotaping and frame-by-frame analysis of the tapes. Illustrative photos were selected to identify the major actions and then special strength, flexibility and explosive exercises were created to duplicate these actions.

The special exercises duplicate each distinct movement so that strength and flexibility are developed in the same movement pattern and range of motion as in running and cutting. In this way, the strength and flexibility that you gain from doing the exercises have an immediate and positive effect on your running and cutting.

For example, in running, once you develop an effective forward thigh drive you will find that your stride length increases and you will be in a better position for a more forceful leg pullback action to give you an even more powerful push-off. The forward knee drive is one of the key speed-producing actions in running, especially in sprinting and when stepping or reaching out with the leg.

The muscles involved in driving the thigh forward are the hip flexors, located in front of the hip. A hip exercise involving these muscles in the same action and range of motion strengthens them in the same way they are used in the run or stepping out. As a result, you learn the feel of the movement as the muscles grow stronger, which in turn enables you to better learn or develop a more effective thigh drive. The increased levels of strength, flexibility and speed of movement give you more control of the thigh movement and at the same time increase your power and speed.

The Yessis System used for improving your abilities consists of three overlapping steps that you must go through. First and foremost is improvement of technique (Step 1). In order to enhance the learning and perfecting of technique, a biomechanical analysis of the running or cutting skill is done first. Corrections are then given for technique deficiencies and, at the same time, specialized strength and flexibility exercises are introduced in order to learn the new movements and make the changes possible. These exercises duplicate what you must do to learn the correct muscle feel and improve the actions that are involved.

As technique is perfected, additional strength and flexibility exercises are introduced to enhance your physical abilities. As you increase your levels of strength and flexibility, not only does your technique become more effective and efficient but your running and cutting speed improves. This is Step 2.

In Step 3, your technique and physical abilities are coupled tightly together and then perfected. Some aspects of speed training are also introduced. At this time you are capable of displaying more effective and efficient technique, which is the basis for further improvement in your functional physical abilities. With an increase in your physical abilities specific to your technique, running speed and speed of executing cutting actions automatically increase. The increases are even more significant when some speed work is added to the workouts. As a result you make the fastest progress possible in relation to developing effective, efficient, and fast running and cutting actions (quickness).

By closely examining each key joint action of the running stride and cutting movement, you will gain a better understanding of each action and how specialized exercises can improve them. This knowledge and its application by you speeds up your improvement greatly. Unfortunately, it takes an injury before most players begin to see the true value of doing exercises specific to running and cutting.

Suzy is a classic example. She was involved in a 3-way collision in mid-field which wrenched her lower back severely and had her arm dislocated at the shoulder when she fell. When she was able to run again, her back hurt so much that she was unable to sprint. I helped her out with exercises specific to the shoulder after her physical therapy ended, and gave her some special exercises to strengthen the lower back. I recommended that she also do some Active Cord (rubber tubing) exercises specific to her running to become even quicker, but she was not interested. As a result, she only did the exercises for the shoulder and lower back.

As she began to see positive results, she slowly began to incorporate running and cutting exercises into her routine. It wasn't long before she began to see dramatic results. Not only was she soon able to run for longer periods of time without getting tired, but she felt much stronger when executing quick sprints to the ball or cuts to get free. According to her, the running and cutting were becoming effortless. She is now a strong believer that only through specialized physical training can a soccer player realize her true potential.

Running and cutting actions and specialized strength and flexibility exercises to develop the muscles as they are used in running and cutting are illustrated and explained in this book. By studying the technique and exercises you will have a better understanding of how this information relates to your personal running and cutting actions. If your running and cutting technique deviates greatly from the most effective technique, then you should modify it for improvement. By doing the strength and flexibility exercises several times a week, you will gain the necessary physical ability and speed of movement required to not only execute the proper mechanics of running and cutting, but to run faster and cut quicker than ever before.

The improvement resulting from these exercises can be quite dramatic. For example, I recently worked with a high school soccer player who also ran on the cross country team. She had good running times but was not exceptional. I analyzed her technique and prescribed specific changes in technique along with a strength training program to develop the muscles needed to improve her technique and enhance her running and cutting actions.

She worked religiously on the exercises, and after about four weeks, began fine-tuning her technique and getting into some speed and explosive training in preparation for competition. During her meets, especially at the cross-country league championships, she was able to place in the top five. What was amazing to her was that she was capable of improving her performance without doing additional running training. In fact, she actually did less running training than she did the previous year. Her soccer playing was also significantly improved and she experienced an important side benefit; it improved her physical appearance.

The same can happen to you. By doing the strength and flexibility exercises that duplicate what occurs in running and cutting, you will be able to develop the strength, flexibility, and explosiveness that you need to improve your game play greatly, much more so than if you only play more.

Although this book contains a great deal of information, I have made a serious attempt to present it in a very simple and straightforward manner. It is well illustrated, not only with actual sequence pictures of players running and cutting, but also with exercises that are specific to the main actions involved in each of these skills. Thus, you should not think of this book as not merely a book on conditioning for soccer; rather, you should approach it as something that will give you a much better understanding of running and cutting and how you can improve your speed and quickness in the shortest amount of time.

You are waiting for the season to begin. Do you wish to attack improvement of your playing skills and performance and do better than ever, or would you rather continue to play the same old way and achieve the same old results? Your success or failure is up to you! If you follow the guidelines presented in this book, I can guarantee you will see outstanding results.

The Role of Specialized Strength and Explosive Exercises

2

All exercises are not equal. It is important to understand the differences between different exercises and especially between specialized and general exercises. There are major differences between them in regard to execution and in the results they produce in your execution of specific skills and game play.

GENERAL STRENGTH EXERCISES

General strength exercises are those exercises that are used in overall body conditioning. They are *not* directly related to the specific actions seen in soccer, (i.e., they do not strengthen the muscles as they are used in running and cutting). They do, however, increase your functional potential for executing these skills.

When the movement pattern in an exercise duplicates what occurs in execution of a specific skill, it is known as a specialized exercise. An example of a specialized exercise for the hamstrings is the pullback (pawback) that is done in the same pathway and in the same range of motion as seen in running, especially in sprinting.

An example of a general exercise is the common leg curl, also known as the hamstring curl. In this exercise you lie face down and bend the knees to bring the shins up toward the thigh. This is an effective exercise for strengthening the hamstring muscle and its tendons that cross the knee joint. It also helps strengthen lateral stability of the knee; but, it does not duplicate any of the forceful actions seen in running or cutting. In running, the shin does fold up behind the thigh after the push-off, but it is more a consequence of the push-off force, not a volitional action.

A key action in running is hip joint extension. This is the main action used in the pawback which drives the leg down and backward to make contact with the ground and as a result, propel the upper body forward. The movement involves the hamstring muscles (together with the gluteus maximus), but, and this is most important, it involves the hamstring muscles and its upper tendons that attach to the hip joint, not the knee joint. It should also be noted that the upper insertion of the hamstring tendons is the site of many hamstring injuries.

Doing the knee curl has little to no effect on the upper junction of the hamstring tendon. Its main outcome is stabilization of the knee flexion action. To be specific to running, you must develop the hamstring muscle as it is used in running, i.e., in hip joint extension, which involves the upper portion of the muscle-tendon arrangement. Thus, hip extension as occurs in the pawback exercise, then becomes a specialized exercise for running. Because hip extension is also an integral part of cutting actions, it can also be used as a specialized exercise for cutting actions.

SPECIALIZED STRENGTH EXERCISES

The key to improving skill execution is to do special exercises that duplicate the movements and actions seen in competitive play. The development of your physical abilities that are specific to soccer skills will have the greatest impact on improving your ability to play more effectively for the entire game. You will see almost immediate results in performance from doing such exercises.

Specialized strength exercises are used to develop not only the physical qualities but also some psychological qualities that apply directly to soccer. The exercises are designed and selected so that the movements and actions closely match those seen in competitive play. Specialized exercises that promote psychological traits consist of movements and actions that require decisiveness, willpower, perseverance and confidence to achieve specific goals. They have similar concentration and psychological qualities as seen during play, especially competitive play.

For example, execution of certain specialized exercises requires deep concentration to develop the neuromuscular pathway needed. A strength exercise that duplicates one aspect of cutting or running requires concentration and perseverance to repeat exactly the same movement pattern time after time so that you develop the necessary muscle feel and are able to repeat it automatically without thinking. For the specialized exercises to have maximum positive transfer you must be decisive in your movements and actions in order to develop the confidence needed to repeat the action during play.

CRITERIA FOR SPECIALIZED STRENGTH EXERCISES

For an exercise to be specific it must fulfill one or more of the following criteria:

1. The exercise must duplicate the exact movement pattern witnessed in the key joint actions involved in cutting and running. For example, an exercise to duplicate the exact ankle, knee, hip or shoulder joint action involved in running or cutting.

2. The exercise must involve the same type of muscular contraction as used in the actual skill. For example, in the push-off in running and cutting, the calf muscles and the Achilles tendon undergo a quick (explosive) shortening contraction (after being pretensed) to produce maximum force. Thus the special exercise must include an explosive muscular contraction as occurs in the ankle joint action, after strength has been developed.

3. The special exercise must develop strength in the same range of motion (ROM) as in competitive play. For example, the thigh raise, in which you raise the thigh directly upward against resistance uses the same muscles as involved in running but not the same ROM as seen in running and cutting actions. More specific to these skills, is to do the thigh drive beginning with the leg behind the body (where it is after the push-off) and then driving the thigh forward rather than upward. The more horizontal the thigh drive is, the greater its contribution to running speed. Thus doing the thigh or knee drive beginning with the leg behind the body, and driving it forward is much more specific to the running and cutting actions. Raising the thigh upward from a standing position is not specific to running and cutting.

The concept of true exercise specificity is new to soccer but the term "specificity" is not. Many authors have used the term "specific exercises" but few exercises described actually fulfill the above criteria. The specificity referred to by these authors usually refers to strengthening or stretching the muscles that may be involved, but not the way they are used in executing specific soccer skills.

For example, it is fairly common to find the Olympic lifts and exercises (snatch, clean and jerk, power clean, etc.) being used as exercises specific to improving soccer skills, especially running and jumping. The Olympic lifts, however, are very specific events and take considerable time to learn well, if they are to be executed with good technique. With poor technique it is common to find many injuries occurring. The weightlifting exercises involve explosive power and are excellent exercises — specific to weightlifting. To say that they are specific to running is erroneous although there may be some transfer to soccer. It should also be noted that weightlifters do not simply do more and more Olympic lifts to improve their performance. They do many other supplementary exercises in addition to perfecting their technique and mastery of the Olympic lifts. The same applies to soccer.

Even the application of valid research data can be deceiving when it comes to specificity of exercise. For example, researchers who conducted electromyographic studies to determine the muscle involvement in running, found that the abdominals play a major role. To strengthen the abdominals the researchers recommended the crunch and the crunch with a twist. These exercises do of course strengthen the abdominals but only through a very small range of motion that is not displayed in sprinting or cutting actions.

When the abdominals come into play in sprinting, it is mainly the abdominal oblique muscles to prevent the hips and shoulders from rotating too much during the run. The obliques also play a major role in rotating the shoulders when cutting. The crunch with a twist involves the obliques but the ROM is extremely small and more importantly, the twisting occurs when the spine is flexed. This is a potentially dangerous situation since rotation of the trunk should always take place when the spine is in correct alignment.

In the crunch exercise it is mainly the upper rectus abdominis that is strengthened. In running and cutting, the lower portion of the rectus abdominis plays the most important role, especially in sprinting. Thus even though the exercises strengthen the abdominals they are not specific to the actual muscle actions involved in running and cutting.

Coaches use many drills for conditioning and improving soccer skills. These drills play a very important role and can enhance physical conditioning and overall game play. But such drills can become more significant and show even greater levels of improvement if you first develop the specific physical and technical abilities needed for the drills. After doing the necessary specialized training, you will be able to execute the skills faster and more effectively for even greater perfection of the actions involved. This will allow you to see the greatest improvement in your overall soccer play.

Typical strength and conditioning programs for soccer usually deal with general exercises to get you "in shape." In some cases, the exercises that are prescribed use the same muscles as used in execution of soccer skills, but if these exercises do not duplicate the same ROM, the same type of muscle contraction, or the exact movement and coordination patterns as seen in running and cutting, they will not be functional, i.e., they will not directly improve these skills.

General conditioning programs and doing general exercises to get in shape can improve your overall playing ability, but not to the extent that specialized exercises can. If you have not weight trained previously, simply getting stronger will enable you to execute the skills more effectively and to play longer without fatigue. For those of you with prior weight training, the improvement in speed and quickness can be even greater when supplemented with explosive (speed-strength) training.

In the sub-teen and teen years, for those who have never weight trained before, simply increasing the levels of strength will show an appreciable difference in your game play. The reason for this is that strength is related to coordination, speed, explosiveness, quickness and endurance. Thus, as you develop strength, you will find yourself more capable of running with better technique and greater speed. You will also be quicker and able to execute many other actions. General strength training has a profound effect on youngsters and those who have not previously weight trained.

For those who have a strong background in weight training, specialized strength training will have the greatest influence. It is at this time that you already have developed basic levels of strength. This is a great foundation for then doing specialized strength exercises that duplicate exactly what you do in your running and cutting actions. In this way you will see much greater improvement in your performance almost immediately, and you will see increases in speed and quickness much faster than if you did only additional running and playing. If you complement or follow-up the specialized strength training with explosive and speed-strength exercises, the improvement in speed and quickness will be even greater. Many girls with whom I have worked are amazed at how much quicker and faster they became in a very short period of time.

Merely getting in shape to prepare yourself for play only brings you up to a level of play that is far below your potential. If you are a teenager, physical maturation can show a significant difference in your playing ability but it is still much less than what you can experience from special training. As an adult, merely getting in shape before the season only enables you to play and, in most cases, not even as well as you did the previous year. Only with supplemental specialized training you can become significantly better each year.

For maximum effectiveness, the development of strength must be in synchronization with your skill development. This is considered usable strength, i.e., the strength that you gain will be displayed in your skill execution. This is the greatest value that specialized exercises can give you that general exercises cannot.

Because of the need for skill duplication, most exercises are best done with elastic tubing as in the Active Cords set, especially for the leg, hip and rotational actions. The reason for this is that it is very difficult and some cases impossible to duplicate the exact movements of the legs, hips and turns with dumbbells, barbells or machines. However, some medicine ball and dumbbell exercises can be of great value.

Another very important reason for using Active Cords, is that almost all of the exercises can be done on the field. This means that you do not have to take an extra trip to the gym and if you do not have much time, you can do the exercises right after practice, as long as you are not in an extreme fatigue state. You can also workout with the exercises at home, in your spare time. All of the exercises do not have to be done at one time and you can spread them out over the day.

Proper Breathing During Specialized Exercises

When you do exercises for technique, strength, speed, or explosiveness, how you breath is very important. Because of this, you should develop proper breathing patterns from the start. This also applies to execution of all soccer skills, ie., jumping, running, dribbling, cutting and kicking.

The instructions for the strength and explosive exercises tell you to inhale and hold your breath on exertion—that is, on the hardest part of the exercise, when you are overcoming resistance. You then exhale on the return, staying in control of the movements. But don't be surprised if you read or hear the opposite from other sources—that you should exhale on exertion and inhale on return.

The widely used recommendation to exhale on exertion is based on theory, not research, and applies mainly to people with heart and circulatory system problems. For example, if you hold your breath for too long (up to eight seconds with a maximal exertion), you could pass out. That is because the internal pressure in the chest and abdomen increases when you hold your breath on exertion. If it increases greatly, it squeezes down on the blood vessels shuttling blood and oxygen to and from the heart. When this happens, you can black out. However, this occurs very rarely, and only on maximum exertion.

If you are without cardiovascular problems and do not hold your breath for more than a few seconds, as needed in the recommended strength exercises, the breath-holding on exertion is perfectly safe. It makes the exercises safer and more effective. If you have high blood pressure or other circulatory system or heart problems, avoid heavy resistance and breath holding. You should also probably not play soccer which is very demanding on the cardiovascular system.

Inhaling and holding the breath briefly on exertion—any exertion, in all sports, including soccer, comes naturally. Many studies have shown that whenever athletic skills are executed properly, athletes hold their breath on the exertion—during the power phase, when maximum force is generated. The breath-holding is especially important when shooting on goal, executing a quick cut on a fast play or accelerating for several yards.

Inhaling and holding the breath on exertion provides up to 20% greater force, stabilizes the spine, and helps prevents lower back injuries. It transforms the trunk (and, in fact, the whole body) into a stable unit against which your hips, shoulders, and arms can move most effectively. In addition, your accuracy improves greatly especially in goal shooting and passing.

Breathing exercises can also help you relax. For example, it is not uncommon to read that you should inhale and then exhale before taking a penalty kick. This is a good technique to help you relax. But before starting the kick, it is important that the muscles have some tension—not excessive tension, but sufficient tension to execute the shot well.

Thus, inhalation and breath-holding are needed immediately before and during execution of the key actions. Studies done with devices to monitor breathing patterns have proven this beyond any doubt. To execute a quick cut, sprint or accurate shot, you must hold your breath during execution.

In effective breathing, especially when you are lifting weights, do not take a maximal breath and then hold it. Doing this can make you very uncomfortable. Just take a breath slightly greater than usual and then hold it to experience the positive benefits. This is especially important for stabilizing the body, holding the spine in position, and getting greater power in your strength exercise or in your running, jumping, cutting and shooting accuracy. Each of these acts is executed very quickly. Breath holding time is very short. Thus, you should have no fear of holding the breath too long or of overexerting yourself.

In regard to stabilization, a few words must be said about the recent trend in the fitness field in regard to core stability and core balance training. Having strong core muscles (abdominal and lower back) is, of course, very important since they play a key role in many soccer skills. In running, your midsection not only holds your body erect but transfers the forces from your legs up through the upper body. Thus, you must have not only a strong core but a flexible midsection for execution of effective cutting actions and to maneuver into position for execution of different kicks and movements.

What is being advocated, is off-balance exercises to develop the stabilization abilities of the muscles. This type of exercise is potentially dangerous and not recommended. If you do most of the exercises with the Active Cords and free weights, you will be developing ample amounts of stabilization strength in order to do the exercises effectively. Many of these "experts" who now advocate this type of training, recommended the use of exercise machines a few years back because you did not have to worry about balance. The machines guided and secured you so that balance did not play a role. They did not recommend the use of free weights which forced you to develop balance with stabilization strength.

They now see the value of such training, but instead of merely recommending the use of free weight exercises, they developed a "new" method of exercising on large round balls and other moveable objects, which are unstable. If you do not have adequate stabilization strength, exercising with them can easily cause injury. In addition, the ROM in most of these exercises is very limited and you will not get much transfer to soccer. Thus, avoid this type of training, which has the potential for injury and contributes very little to your abilities. Doing the exercises presented in this book will more than suffice to develop your ability to balance and stabilize yourself during the execution of various skills.

Analysis of Running Technique

3

To improve your running speed, the prevalent philosophy is to do more running. It is strongly believed that by doing more running, especially on an intense level, you not only improve speed and quickness but you also get in shape to play the game. This is why many players usually run before, and/or after playing and do so on a year-round basis as opposed to doing supplementary strength and explosive training.

Doing more running to improve running speed and quickness often leads to injuries, especially if you have poor running technique. This is why on any given day it is not uncommon to find many players coming down with injuries sustained while running in practice or during play. Although weight training is sometimes considered as a way to prevent such injuries it should more accurately be classified as supplemental training since its main purpose should be to improve your running speed and quickness. Injury prevention is secondary, especially when you consider that most injuries are due to poor neuromuscular coordination (technique) ie., the biomechanics of how you run and execute changes in direction and other skills.

Even though soccer players have generally relied more on the quantity of running rather than the quality of running, by taking a little time to improve the quality of your running will you be able to run faster and longer. Your chances of injury will also be diminished and you will have improved your agility. With better technique, you will be able to cut faster and be much quicker in your overall playing. These are the outstanding traits of high-level players.

Changes in how you run can usually be made quite easily. The higher the level of your neuromuscular skill and the more developed your physical abilities, the easier it is to make changes. For example, many of the soccer players shown in this book were able to make changes very quickly. They were good players (most were national champions in the 17 and under age bracket), and had good coordination. By telling them what had to be done and showing them how to execute the correct movements, they were able to make changes so that the new technique became automatic. The key point here is that you can change technique to make your running (and other soccer skills) more economical and mechanically sound. By improving your physical qualities you can make these changes easier, faster and more effective.

Through biomechanics and kinesiology it is possible to determine what constitutes good running technique and why such technique is effective. In essence you learn the best way to run and why it is the best way to run for soccer. In addition you learn how effective running helps to prevent injury. Still another way that biomechanics and kinesiology can help to improve your running, especially sprinting, is through analysis and understanding of each of the main elements (actions) involved and how they are executed. Once effective technique or execution of the key joint actions is known, it is then possible to use exercises that duplicate these exact movements. In this way the gains in strength, flexibility and other physical factors will have a direct effect on your running.

RUNNING SPECIFICS

Before getting into the specific details of running technique it must be pointed out that it is rare to find a soccer player with perfect running technique including the world's best players. (It is also rare to find some of the best sprinters in the world with perfect running technique.) Each player has very strong positive aspects to her running technique which typically enable her to become a great fast break artist or someone who can outrun her opponent going down the field.

The figures you see in this book are of mostly excellent soccer players who have won league or national competititons. However, not one of them can be used to illustrate each positive aspect of the most effective running sprint. Thus when you are referred to particular figures, look at the frames in question to see the positive or well-executed portions of the technique. When you look at other aspects of the running technique know that they can be improved.

I have looked at the running technique of thousands of players and have worked with many of them. I have found that every player regardless of her level of ability can improve her running technique and speed. This is true regardless of whether you are already the best on your team, best in your state or even in the nation. For example, even the winning Olympic team women could have improved their speed and quickness with better technique.

For effective running technique in soccer it is not necessary that you duplicate the best technique of a world class sprinter. Most important in soccer is to be able to execute quick bursts of speed to get by your opponent when executing a fast break or not allowing your opponent to out-run you. Also important is to be able to run effectively the entire game without undue fatigue.

To achieve both greater speed and to prevent early fatigue it is important that you have effective technique. The better your technique the easier it is to run and the more economical is your running. This not only gets you from one point to another faster but also allows you to do it more often without unnecessary fatigue. Keep in mind that the more economical your running, the less fatigued you become and the more capable you are of executing a good pass, shot on goal or a defensive maneuver after a sprint.

In the following biomechanical analysis of running technique I bring out the key aspects of running technique that you can incorporate to make you faster with the least amount of effort.

Running technique can best be described in three phases: *push-off*, *flight*, and *support*. For the push-off, see Figure 3.1 frames 2-3 and 9-11, Figure 3.2 frames 2-4 and 10-12, Figure 3.3 frames 3-5, and Figure 3.4 frames 3-5. For the flight phase, see Figure 3.1 frames 4-6, Figure 3.2 frames 4-6, Figure 3.3 frames 5-7, and Figure 3.4 frames 5-7. For the support phase see Figure 3.1 frames 7-8, Figure 3.2 frames 7-9 and Figure 3.4 frames 8-10.

The push-off (technically the second half of the support phase) is used mainly to create greater horizontal force for speed and to get you airborne. In the flight phase, you utilize the forces generated in the push-off to cover the optimal, but not maximal, distance. In addition, you prepare for touchdown (ground contact). The support phase, which occurs as soon as the foot makes contact with the ground, is used mainly to support the body, to not allow excessive up and down motions and to prepare the muscles and tendons for the push-off.

RUNNING TECHNIQUE (figures 3-1)

Figure 3.1-1

Figure 3.1-2 (push-off)

Figure 3.1-3 (push-off)

Figure 3.1-7 (support)

Figure 3.1-8 (support)

Figure 3.1-9 (push-off)

Figure 3.1-13

Figure 3.1-4 (flight)

Figure 3.1-5 (flight)

Figure 3.1-6 (flight)

Figure 3.1-10 (push-off)

Figure 3.1-11 (push-off)

Figure 3.1-12

RUNNING TECHNIQUE (figures 3-2)

Figure 3.2-1

Figure 3.2-2 (push-off)

Figure 3.2-3 (push-off)

Figure 3.2-7 (support)

Figure 3.2-8 (support)

Figure 3.2-9 (support)

Figure 3.2-13

Figure 3.2-14

Figure 3.2-15

Figure 3.2-4 (flight)

Figure 3.2-5 (flight)

Figure 3.2-6 (flight)

Figure 3.2-10 (push-off)

Figure 3.2-11 (push-off)

Figure 3.2-12 (push-off)

RUNNING TECHNIQUE *(figures 3-3)*

Figure 3.3-1

Figure 3.3-2

Figure 3.3-3 (push-off)

Figure 3.3-7 (flight)

Figure 3.3-8

Figure 3.3-9

Figure 3.3-13

Figure 3.3-14

Figure 3.3-15

Figure 3.3-4 (push-off)

Figure 3.3-5 (flight)

Figure 3.3-6 (flight)

Figure 3.3-10

Figure 3.3-11

Figure 3.3-12

RUNNING TECHNIQUE (figures 3-4)

Figure 3.4-1

Figure 3.4-2

Figure 3.4-3

Figure 3.4-7

Figure 3.4-8

Figure 3.4-9

Figure 3.4-13

Figure 3.4-14

Figure 3.4-15

Figure 3.4-4   Figure 3.4-5   Figure 3.4-6

Figure 3.4-10   Figure 3.4-11   Figure 3.4-12

Figure 3.4-16

THE PUSH-OFF

The push-off involves one major joint action: ankle extension. The more powerful the ankle joint extension, the greater the forward driving force that can be generated. Understand that knee joint extension is used only when starting to run. If the push-off (support) leg straightens fully you are leaping, not running. Straightening the support push-off leg fully also requires greater energy and gives you more of a vertical rather than a horizontal force component. The more horizontally the push-off force is applied, the faster is your running. Thus, as the ankle joint extension takes place, the knee of your push-off leg remains firm, in a slightly bent position. (See Figure 3.1 frame 3, Figure 3.3 frames 5 and 12, Figure 3.4 frames 4 and 5, and Figure 3.5 frames 5 and 12.) Some knee extension may take place, not to propel you forward, but to raise the body up again from the crouch during support. It should take place as your body moves out in front of the support leg .

As you push-off, the swing leg thigh continues to be forcefully driven forward and there is full ankle joint extension so that you are on "tip toe". The swing leg thigh is driven through forcefully, by an initial forceful contraction of the hip flexor muscles (iliopsoas, pectineus and rectus femoris) when the leg is behind the body (after the pushoff). (See Figure 3.1 frames 4-11, Figure 3.2 frames 5-11, and Figure 3.3 frames 6-11.) The more forceful the initial muscular contraction, the higher the thigh will rise (usually 55-75 degrees from the vertical). (See Figure 3.1 frames 3 and 11, Figure 3.2 frame 4, and Figure 3.5 frame 4.) The knee drive, which starts in the flight phase and continues during the landing and the push-off, is a key force producing action. It contributes greatly to producing more speed. The key is to drive the knee (thigh) forward not upward!

In a powerful knee drive, which is the key to speed in sprinting, the heel gets close to the buttocks when the thigh is angled forward! (See Figure 3.1 frame 8, Figure 3.5 frame 9, and Figure 3.6 frame 9.) This folding of the leg, coupled with the knee drive is very safe. If the thigh is vertical when the heel is close to the buttocks (i.e., when you "kick your butt" as in Figure 3.2 frame 8, and Figure 3.9 frame 2) the hamstrings would be working when they should be relaxing. This slows you down and leads to hamstring pulls. Also, it requires excessive flexibility of the quadriceps muscle which can be dangerous to the knee.

The arm bends at the elbow and moves forward in front of the body until the hand is about chest or shoulder high. The elbow bends to about a 90-degree or less angle during the forward drive. (See Figure 3.1 frames 6-11, Figure 3.2 frames 1-4, and Figure 3.3 frames 6-11.) When the arm moves backward, it straightens in synchronization with the leg contacting the ground. (See Figure 3.1 frame 1, Figure 3.2 frame 9, Figure 3.4 frame 9, and Figure 3.6 frame 2.) This action is often forceful to create greater landing forces and a stronger push-off. When the arm actions are coordinated with the leg actions, the arm straightens and stops momentarily in synchronization with the support leg. When the arm bends and is driven forward, it is in synchronization with the forward bent knee thigh drive.

FLIGHT (AIRBORNE) PHASE

The flight phase is about as long as the support phase. The more frequently the foot is in contact with the ground, the more force it can generate to continually drive you forward. But there must be a flight phase to use the force that has been generated in the push-off and thigh and arm drives.

To prepare for touchdown during flight, the shin swings out as the thigh drive slows down and stops to create a straight leg. A slight lowering of the thigh may also occur to facilitate the swing out of the shin and leg straightening (see Figure 3.1 frames 2-5, and Figure 3.5 frames 3-6 and 11-14.) As the leg is fully straightened, it is driven down and back to create more force when it makes contact with the ground. This action entails use of the hamstring and gluteus maximus muscles and is known as pawback (see Figure 3.1 frames 5-7 and Figure 3.5 frames 6-8 and 14-16).

To ensure that you have the shortest lever possible when the shin swings out (which gives you greater speed of shin movement), you must raise the toe part of the foot (dorsiflex the ankle) (see Figure 3.3 frames 1-6 and Figure 3.5 frames 1-6). This foot position is also needed to enable you to land more on the ball of the foot or mid-foot when you bring the leg down and back. If you kept the foot pointed (ankle extended), as it is after the push-off, not only would it take longer to swing the leg out in front, but you would make contact with the ground early, well in front of the body. Ideally, the touchdown should be closer to the vertical projection of your center of gravity.

Thus the ankle dorsiflexion plays an important role not only to increase speed of movement of the shin but to ensure an effective landing. In most players, this action seems to occur naturally. If it doesn't, take steps to correct it! This is especially true of some players who develop the extended foot (pointed toes) habit because of the kicks that they execute. But to be a great player, you must develop the ability to switch as the need arises.

In regard to economy, the shin does not fold up completely behind the thigh. Most important is that the shin be behind the length of the thigh (between two perpendicular-to-the-thigh lines, one at the knee and one at the hip). The slightly above level position of the shin during the forward drive saves energy by not having to contract the hamstring muscles to raise the shin higher (see Figure 3.1 frames 4-8, Figure 3.3 frames 6-10 and Figure 3.5 frames 6-9).

The shin must be sufficiently above level so that the foot is "hidden" behind the length of the thigh. When you sprint, because of the great forces generated in the push-off, the heel rises higher so that it comes close to the buttocks. This should occur only when the knee is in front of the body. You should not "kick" yourself in the butt. This is a wasteful and potentially dangerous action.

When the backward moving foot contacts the ground and stops, the upper body continues to move forward. This major action, known as pawback, contributes greatly to forward speed. When sprinting, the leg should be brought back very forcefully so that ground contact is directly under the body on the ball of the foot or ball-heel immediately. Without pawback or with very little pawback, landing takes place slightly in front of the body on mid-foot or heel-ball immediately (see Figure 3.8 frames 6-9, Figure 3.7 frames 7-8, and Figure 3.9 frames 7-8).

Lack of pawback is one of the most common sprinting problems that I see among soccer players that have basically good push-offs and fair knee drives, but, instead of swinging the swing leg out and back, they simply lower the leg to make contact with the ground. When this happens, the trail leg is too far behind the body which then takes longer to come forward before the push-off. Also, they get no force out of the leg when it comes in contact with the ground; instead it slows them down because of the braking forces. Not only does the forward plant act as a brake to forward speed, but they do not get any additional force from the backward moving leg to propel the upper body forward.

The closer the foot lands to the vertical projection of the body's center of mass (directly under the body) the less are the braking forces. This is the main reason why the heel hit is so inefficient in running (see Figure 3.2 frames 6 and 13, and Figure 3.8 frames 7-8). When you land on your heel in front of your body, it momentarily stops your forward motion because of the great forces created against your forward motion. These forces which can be up to 10 times your body weight are the culprit in many leg, hip and even lower back injuries. To eliminate the braking forces as much as possible, it is important that the leg be moving backwards as it makes contact with the ground.

The backward leg movement and the following ground contact are very important in continuing the fast forward movement of the upper body. At ground contact, the upper body continues to move in front of the support leg so that when the push-off occurs the body will be out in front as far as possible (see Figure 3.1 frames 3 and 11, and Figure 3.2 frame 4). In this way the push-off is directed more in a horizontal direction rather than projecting the body more vertically (upward) as typically occurs when the heel contacts the ground first with the foot angled upward.

When you land with a heel hit, the whole foot must then come down to make contact with the ground. Thus, it takes longer for the upper body to move over the foot. As a result, when you then push-off, the body is not as far forward as possible and you have a strong vertical push-off component. Because of this, the heel hit prevents you from sprinting at top speed as well as being potentially injurious because of the high landing forces.

When you want to stop forward motion, the heel hit is very effective. By fully extending the leg out in front and making contact with the ground on the heel, you block, or stop your lower body movement. In sprinting, you do not want the heel hit; use it only to execute a stop or backward change in direction.

SUPPORT PHASE

The support phase, also known as the phase of amortization, begins when the foot makes contact with the ground and ends when you break contact with the ground at the end of the push-off (take-off). The body is in full support on the leg immediately after initial contact is made and your leg bends slightly to absorb some of the forces, but mainly to withstand the forces in order to accumulate energy for the push-off. Half of the support time is for the landing and half is for the push-off. In world-class sprinters, this phase lasts less than 0.1 sec; 0.5 sec for amortization (cushioning and tension build-up) and .05 sec for the take-off! (See Figures 3.1-3.9.)

The major support phase occurs when the foot is in full contact with the ground and your upper body weight is over the support leg. The leg muscles at this time are used mainly to hold you upright (to prevent "sitting"). The more up and down motion you have in running, the more energy you expend, and the less efficient is the run. Note that in world-class sprinters, the amount of up and down motion of their center of mass is only about one inch! Thus if your leg support muscles are

RUNNING TECHNIQUE (figures 3-5)

Figure 3.5-1

Figure 3.5-2

Figure 3.5-3

Figure 3.5-7

Figure 3.5-8

Figure 3.5-9

Figure 3.5-13

Figure 3.5-14

Figure 3.5-15

Figure 3.5-4   Figure 3.5-5   Figure 3.5-6

Figure 3.5-10   Figure 3.5-11   Figure 3.5-12

Figure 3.5-16

RUNNING TECHNIQUE (figures 3-6)

Figure 3.6-1

Figure 3.6-2

Figure 3.6-3

Figure 3.6-4

Figure 3.6-5

Figure 3.6-6

Figure 3.6-7

Figure 3.6-8

Figure 3.6-9

RUNNING TECHNIQUE *(figures 3-7)*

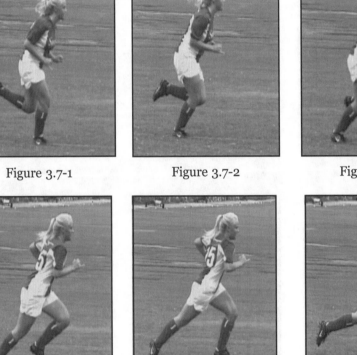

Figure 3.7-1   Figure 3.7-2   Figure 3.7-3

Figure 3.7-4   Figure 3.7-5   Figure 3.7-6

Figure 3.7-7   Figure 3.7-8   Figure 3.7-9

RUNNING TECHNIQUE (figures 3-8)

Figure 3.8-1

Figure 3.8-2

Figure 3.8-3

Figure 3.8-4

Figure 3.8-5

Figure 3.8-6

Figure 3.8-7

Figure 3.8-8

Figure 3.8-9

RUNNING TECHNIQUE (figures 3-9)

Figure 3.9-1

Figure 3.9-2

Figure 3.9-3

Figure 3.9-4

Figure 3.9-5

Figure 3.9-6

Figure 3.9-7

Figure 3.9-8

Figure 3.9-9

weak and allow you to "sink" too much after touchdown, you must use up extra energy to raise the body, which can then bring on early fatigue.

The following example shows how much energy can be expended over the course of a game. If you lifted your body higher by even a quarter of an inch, i.e., one additional quarter of an inch of vertical lift in every push-off, you would be doing the equivalent of work required to lift your body mass to the height of a five-story building! This extra work performed during the game is very uneconomical and has a strong negative influence on your running speed, quickness, and body energy. Thus, the more horizontally your body moves in running, the greater will be your speed and the less fatigue you will experience.

To prevent excessive flexion in the knee during support, the quadriceps femoris muscle on the anterior thigh undergoes a strong eccentric contraction. When the tension is sufficiently great, downward movement stops at which point the quadriceps contract isometrically to hold the leg position. If this muscle is weak you will have excessive lowering

RUNNING TECHNIQUE (figures 3-10)

Figure 3.10-1

Figure 3.10-2

Figure 3.10-3

Figure 3.10-4

Figure 3.10-5

Figure 3.10-6

of the body and greater energy expenditure. Also, if you do not make contact close to mid-foot or on the ball of the foot, the leg and foot muscles and tendons will not be able to withstand any of the landing forces. These structures are very important for the initial shock absorption as is tensing the muscles and tendons on the plantar (under) surface of the foot and lower leg. At the same time the ankle, knee and hip joints undergo slight flexion to help absorb some of the landing forces but most importantly, the muscles and tendons withstand the landing forces and accumulate energy as the muscles tense up during their stretch.

Stretching of the Achilles' and other tendons is very important for creating energy in the push-off. Note that as the tendons are forcefully and quickly stretched (in effective contact with the ground) the greater is the tension developed in the tendons and associated muscles. The energy stored in this tension is then given back in the push-off. If all the forces were absorbed there would be no energy to give back in the push-off. Thus there should only be enough absorption to cushion you and to help prevent injury on initial contact. Also, if you do not make contact on the midfoot but instead land on the heel, the Achilles' tendon would not be able to absorb or withstand any of the landing forces. As a result the forces travel up the body and become potentially dangerous. More importantly, you would not be able to create or store energy for the push-off.

THE ARM ACTIONS

In effective and safe running the arm actions coordinate (synchronize) with the leg actions. When running "slowly" (at a five or more minute mile pace), the arms are held at approximately a 90-degree angle in the elbows to economize energy. The elbow is raised to the rear during the backswing phase of the arm action while the opposite arm is brought forward to synchronize with the thigh drive. The elbow rises approximately 45 degrees to the rear as it mimics the range of motion in the hip joint (see Figure 3.8 frame 5).

The arms should move basically in a forward/backward motion so that all the driving forces move in a straight line forward (see Figures 3.11 and 3.13). If your shoulders rotate (turn sideways), the arms may appear to cross the body, but in reality they do not (see Figure 3.10 frame 3, and Figure 3.12 frame 3). If you see your hands coming across the body, check to see if it is due to the shoulder rotation or if your elbows flare out to the sides or both.

In sprinting, there should be a powerful forward drive of the arm when the elbow is flexed 90-degrees after being straightened on the back

RUNNING TECHNIQUE (figures 3-11)

Figure 3.11-1

Figure 3.11-2

Figure 3.11-3

Figure 3.11-4

Figure 3.11-5

swing. The arm flexes and moves forward until the elbow is alongside or just slightly in front of the body. There is approximately a 90-degree bend in the elbow and the hand is about chest to shoulder high (see Figure 3.1 frame 10, Figure 3.2 frame 5, and Figure 3.3 frame 11). The arm then straightens as it moves back and down so that when the arm is alongside of the body it is relatively straight (see Figure 3.1 frame 1, Figure 3.2 frame 9, Figure 3.6 frame 2, and Figure 3.9 frame 3). The long lever of the arm is needed to slow it down so that it synchronizes with the leg stopping when the foot is in contact with the ground.

After the arm is straightened, the elbow is raised to the rear. This action bends the elbow and prepares it for being driven forward in synchronization with the bent leg forward knee drive (see Figure 3.2 frames 11-12 and Figure 3.4 frames 10-13). This combination of actions gives you efficient arm and leg movement and thus contributes to greater speed.

RUNNING TECHNIQUE (figures 3-12)

Figure 3.12-1

Figure 3.12-2

Figure 3.12-3

Figure 3.12-4

Figure 3.12-5

Figure 3.12-6

The arms play a very important role in keeping the shoulders square to the direction of running which in turn, helps to keep the hips square so that the thighs move directly forward and backward. If your hips turn sideways, your foot plant may show a zig-zag pattern which directs the push-off forces somewhat to the sides rather than directly forward. Figures 3.10, 3.12 and 3.15 show slight hip rotation which is counteracted by the shoulder rotation.

In order for the shoulders and hips to remain square (facing forward), you must have strong abdominal oblique muscles, in addition to strong lower back rotational muscles. Your shoulders and neck should be relaxed even when striving to run faster and with increasing fatigue. If these muscles become tense you will be very tight across the neck and shoulders which not only brings on greater fatigue, but it restricts effective arm movement.

OTHER IMPORTANT ASPECTS OF TECHNIQUE

One of the most important features of sprinting is the forceful forward drive of the thigh. The faster the thigh comes forward, the greater your stride length and the better the preparation for a forceful pawback movement. This in turn makes it possible to complete each stride more quickly which, in turn, increases stride frequency. For cutting, the knee drive is very important in having a quick and powerful first stride or to quickly step out especially when in a ready position.

In sprinting, the knee is brought forward and then backward at maximum speed so that when ground contact is made you will see only one thigh when viewed from the side (see Figure 3.5 frame 9). In other words, the forward moving thigh lines up with the backward moving thigh as full contact with the ground takes place. In some cases the swing leg is driven forward so forcefully it may be slightly in front of the support thigh. If it is slightly behind, as in Figure 3.1 frame 7 and Figure 3.2 frame 8, it indicates the need for a stronger, more powerful thigh drive.

When on a fast break (sprinting), the exact amount of separation between the thighs at the moment of foot contact is not critical. The key element here is that the forward swing leg moves in front of the body and then moves backward (pawback) prior to good contact. This not

RUNNING TECHNIQUE (figures 3-13)

Figure 3.13-1   Figure 3.13-2   Figure 3.13-3   Figure 3.13-4

Figure 3.13-5   Figure 3.13-6   Figure 3.13-7

RUNNING TECHNIQUE (figures 3-14)

Figure 3.14-1

Figure 3.14-2

Figure 3.14-3

Figure 3.14-4   Figure 3.14-5

only decreases the amount of braking forces, but increases your stride length and increases your acceleration.

The hands and fingers should remain relaxed at all times. The wrist should be relaxed and loose and held basically in the neutral position. In sprinting, it is even possible to see the hand literally "flapping" during the run which is indicative of high levels of relaxation. Seeing a fist or locked fingers is indicative of tension.

The position of your head and where you focus your vision govern not only your body position, but also your body balance. Be sure you have good posture with your head directly above the shoulders, which should be directly above the hips which are directly above the feet when in full stride. When accelerating, as occurs most often in soccer play, there will be a slight forward lean of the trunk. This is needed for a quick burst of speed for five to ten yards. If you must go further, you should then get into the erect posture for a full stride.

RUNNING TECHNIQUE (figures 3-15)

Figure 3.15-1   Figure 3.15-2   Figure 3.15-3

Figure 3.15-4   Figure 3.15-5

You should always look directly forward or on a level plane if looking left or right. You should not look down as does the player in Figure 3.8. If your head is forward you will find yourself leaning forward excessively which uses even more energy to maintain balance. This can be seen clearly in Figure 3.7. Leaning forward should only be used when accelerating! (Note that in Figure 3.7, the initial acceleration was already completed.)

A common sign of tension is facial strain. To determine if you are tense when running, smile every so often. If you feel a distinct change in your features (or in your body), then you know that you have tension. Do this often to check if your body is relaxed. The more relaxed the non-running muscles are, the more effective your running technique becomes and the less the energy that you use. But, if you are too relaxed you will not be able to run well. Some tension is needed for good posture and effective muscle action.

WARMING UP BEFORE RUNNING AND PLAYING

To get ready for running and playing, you should do some active stretches and jogging and then begin practicing some of the game skills. For most players, this is sufficient and they feel ready to perform. Others merely like to begin doing some of the game skills or simply begin playing after an easy jog. To truly prepare your body, especially the muscles for running, cutting and playing, it is important that the muscles be thoroughly warmed up before all-out performances. For some of the best stretches that you can do at this time, see Chapter 7.

To make needed changes in technique, it is necessary to know exactly what you are doing in your running and cutting actions. For this, it is important to have a biomechanical and kinesiological analysis of your technique. For information on how to film yourself and how to get an individualized analysis and exercise program based on your technique, please see the information on how to contact Sports Training, Inc. in the back of this book.

4

Agility: Analysis of Cutting Actions

In soccer, speed is one of the most important physical qualities. However, in many situations, agility, the key to quickness, may be equal to, if not more important than speed. Agility, sometimes known as maneuverability, is the ability to change direction of the body or body parts as quickly as possible while in motion. When you execute the change in direction while running, it is known as a cutting action. The ability to make these changes in direction (cutting actions) quickly and sharply is the key to being able to successfully execute many soccer-specific skills.

For example, being able to make quick, sharp cuts in direction while in motion, is the key to being able to elude your opponent when on offense, and to keep up with your opponent on defense. Making quick changes in any direction is the key to getting free to receive a pass, to make a shot, or simply to stay with your opponent when she makes a fast break. By becoming more agile and quicker in your movements, the better all-round player you can become. Development of this ability is especially rewarding when you are able to elude your opponent and open yourself up for a pass or to make a successful shot on goal.

THE KEY COMPONENTS OF AGILITY

In order to make a change in direction while in motion, especially a quick one, you must have adequate levels of strength (eccentric, concentric and isometric), speed-strength (explosive strength), flexibility (range of motion-ROM) and coordination (technique). Also included is reaction time and speed of movement which is related to your strength levels. Each of these components can be improved separately and in combination with one another. As you improve these abilities, you can learn more effective movements and improve your ability to execute the movements quickly. These abilities are exhibited in all forms of dodging, zig-zag running, stopping and starting, moving in different directions quickly and sharply, changing body positions, and moving the limbs and body into different positions quickly. By improving each of these key components you can improve your overall agility.

For many players, agility is the key to their success, especially when they don't have exceptional speed or the ability to accomplish other important game skills. Of all the physical qualities needed for better agility, coordination (effective technique) is most important in the early stages of training. Once you learn how to execute the movements and can do them well, you will see a major difference in your performance. Once technique is mastered, improvement in your physical abilities becomes most important.

Strength, especially eccentric strength, the key to your ability to successfully stop motion in one direction and to generate the force needed to quickly move out in another direction, is most important. Your eccentric strength prepares the muscles for an explosive contraction. Thus the greater your eccentric muscle strength and the greater your ability to quickly switch from an eccentric to the concentric contraction, the more power (explosiveness) you will be able to exhibit in your speed and quickness.

Reaction time becomes important when you must deal with your opponent's actions. You must be able to pick up cues from your opponent as to when she is going to make a change in direction, and then be able to quickly go into action to keep up with or out-perform her. Thus speed of movement and reaction time are closely intertwined. Of the two, speed of movement can be increased the most.

GENERAL CHARACTERISTICS OF A CUTTING ACTION

Before you can change direction, it is necessary to stop your motion in the direction in which you are moving. The faster you are running, the more difficult this becomes and your ability to make a sharp change in direction diminishes. However, the stronger you are, the faster you can go and the quicker you can stop your movement in one direction and make a sharp change in direction. This is how improving your physical abilities can improve your performance greatly.

To stop your forward motion you must have sufficient eccentric strength, also known as stopping strength. In essence, the quadriceps muscle of the leg undergoes a strong stretch and develops tension as the

CUTTING ACTION (figures 4-1)

Figure 4.1-1

Figure 4.1-2

Figure 4.1-3

Figure 4.1-4

Figure 4.1-5

Figure 4.1-6

Figure 4.1-7

Figure 4.1-8

Figure 4.1-9

CUTTING ACTION (figures 4-2)

Figure 4.2-1

Figure 4.2-2

Figure 4.2-3

Figure 4.2-4

Figure 4.2-5

Figure 4.2-6

Figure 4.2-7

Figure 4.2-8

Figure 4.2-9

knee bends after you place the leg out in front and/or side to stop forward motion. The initial landing takes place on the heel or on the inside border of the foot followed by the whole foot as your weight comes over this forward plant leg. As the quadriceps muscle and its tendon stretch (lengthen), they develop greater tension and when the tension becomes sufficiently great, the knee bending stops, which in turn stops the lowering of your body. The less the lowering of the body and the faster you stop your forward motion, the more effective the cutting action which enables you to move out in a new direction more quickly.

When you plant (stick) the forward leg to stop your motion, it should always be placed in a direction opposite the one in which you intend to move, especially for a sharp change. For example, if you wish to execute a cutting action to your right, you must plant the left leg out to the side to your left (see Figures 4.1 and 4.2). The plant may also be slightly in front of the body depending upon the direction and speed of your approach (see Figures 4.8 and 4.9). Note that the foot plant must be sufficiently forceful so that you "stick" your foot in place to prevent slipping and to load the muscles. The harder the foot hits the ground the more you can create muscle tension in the muscles as needed for a quick push-off.

A forward and to the left foot plant when moving forward allows you to stop your forward motion and at the same time to place you in an advantageous position to move out to the right (see Figures 4.8 and 4.9). However, keep in mind that the cutting action cannot be sharp if you are running very fast. Thus if you anticipate making a sharp 90° cut to the side, you must slow down your speed accordingly so that you can execute the change in direction. If the cut is angled about 45-60 degrees to the side then your forward motion can be faster (see Figures 4.11 and 4.12).

As your foot firmly contacts the ground, you lower your body (weight) to become more stable and to make the stopping action more powerful. Keep in mind that the more you lower your body, the more stable (resistant to movement) your body becomes. This in turn then allows you to make a change and to move out in another direction. The taller (higher) you remain, the more difficult a change in motion becomes. In this case, when making a quick stop in one step, there will be a greater tendency to lean over your stopping leg or you will have to take two or more steps to stop.

Thus, if you want to stop quickly, you must get the body low. The lowering of the body is usually done by taking a wide step out to the side, front or a combination of both and then bending the stopping leg to lower the body while still keeping the trunk erect (see Figures 4.2 frame 3 and 4.3 frame 3). How well you do this depends on your hip joint flexibility and leg strength. Note that in Figure 4.5, she also bends at the waist to get low. This is inefficient and it takes longer to execute the cut.

If you are on offense and wish to elude your opponent, you should look your opponent in the eye as you step out to stop and lower your body. By looking at your opponent, it will take her longer to realize that you are about to make a change in direction. This does not preclude your ability to execute feinting actions (as for example, first turning your head in the opposite direction) to fool your opponent.

CUTTING ACTION (figures 4-3)

Figure 4.3-1

Figure 4.3-2

Figure 4.3-3

Figure 4.3-4

Figure 4.3-5

Figure 4.3-6

Figure 4.3-7

Figure 4.3-8

Figure 4.3-9

Figure 4.3-10

Figure 4.3-11

CUTTING ACTION (figures 4-4)

Figure 4.4-1

Figure 4.4-2

Figure 4.4-3

Figure 4.4-4

Figure 4.4-5

Figure 4.4-6

Figure 4.4-7

Figure 4.4-8

Figure 4.4-9

Figure 4.4-10

Figure 4.4-11

CUTTING ACTION (figures 4-5)

Figure 4.5-1

Figure 4.5-2

Figure 4.5-3

Figure 4.5-4

Feinting actions are effective, but you should learn to mix them up. For example, look your opponent straight in the eye with no movement of the head for one cut and in another, turn the head in one direction and then cut to the opposite side. The more you can change how you execute feints, the more off-balance you can keep your opponent and the more effective your movements will become.

To execute a cutting action, as you forcefully stick the leg on the ground turn the foot so that the sole is perpendicular to the direction in which you want to move. You should also begin to turn the hips together with

CUTTING ACTION (figures 4-6)

Figure 4.6-1

Figure 4.6-2

Figure 4.6-3

Figure 4.6-4

Figure 4.6-5

Figure 4.6-6

Figure 4.6-7

Figure 4.6-8

Figure 4.6-9

Figure 4.6-10

Figure 4.6-11

the plant foot when making a sideways change. If you are running for-ward and want to cut to the left or right the hips should remain facing forward during the foot plant.

When your stopping leg is anchored, your inside non-cutting (swing) leg should be off the ground and free to move out (see Figures 4.1, frame 3, 4.2 frame 5, and 4.3, frame 6). Your head and shoulders should remain facing forward so that your opponent cannot read any anticipated changes in your actions since she will still be looking you in the eye or watching your upper body.

As your stopping action ends, begin the push-off in the new direc-tion and at the same time begin to turn your trunk and swing leg in the intended direction of movement. At this time, you step out with the non-support (swing) leg in the new direction in preparation for move-ment in the new direction (see Figures 4.1, frames 3-4, and 4.8 frame 6).

Note that as your weight is concentrated on the stopping (outside) leg, the inside swing leg is unweighted and allowed to move freely. As you step out and place the swing leg foot on the ground for running in the new direction, the foot and lower body should be turned into the new direction. The rear foot breaks contact with the ground as you move forward in the new direction with a running stride (see Figures 4.1, 4.3, 4.8-4.10). After one or more steps, you should be ready to stop and ex-ecute another cut, kick or receive the ball or speed up your movements depending on the play action.

SPECIFIC CUTTING ACTIONS

Basic cutting technique is the same regardless of whether you are running forward and wish to cut to one or the other side, if you want to make an angled cut while still continuing in a forward direction or if you want to go forward and backward as quickly as possible. The same basic technique also applies to running sideways and then changing di-rection to run to the opposite side. In essence, each of these different types of cuts include a body stopping and lowering phase, sequential body turning actions and a push-off, all executed in one step. More specifically, the actions involved in each type of cutting action are as follows:

Side to Side Cutting Actions

A side to side shuttle step when moving laterally is effective when speed and quickness is not of major importance or when you are adjust-ing to the movements of your opponents before you go into action. But,

RUNNING TECHNIQUE (figures 4-7)

Figure 4.7-1

Figure 4.7-2

Figure 4.7-3

Figure 4.7-7

Figure 4.7-8

Figure 4.7-9

Figure 4.7-13

Figure 4.7-14

Figure 4.7-4   Figure 4.7-5   Figure 4.7-6

Figure 4.7-10   Figure 4.7-11   Figure 4.7-12

to move laterally for quickness using a cutting action as described above is much more effective.

When running in a sideways direction, you should be in a regular running stride with the hips and legs while the head and shoulders face forward to keep your eyes focused on the play action. To be able to do this, you must have the necessary midsection flexibility, i.e., be able to rotate the hips 90 degrees while the shoulders remain in place. **Note that the players in most of the cinematograms (even high-level players) do not have the flexibility to do this!** (See Figures 4.1-4.7.) Gaining the necessary strength and flexibility will help them tremendously.

EXECUTION AND LEARNING PROGRESSION

- From a walk or slow jog, plant the outside leg out to the side on the inner border of the foot to stop your sideward motion (see Figure 4.2 frames 2-4).

- Lower your weight by bending the leg and dropping the hips but still maintain a front facing position with the head and shoulders. As you bend the support leg, raise the inside leg off the ground. It should be relaxed and able to swing freely (see Figure 4.3 frames 5-6, and Figure 4.5 frame 4).

- As soon as body lowering has ceased, push-off with the stopping leg and step out with the inside swing leg in the new direction. Turn the hips to the new direction of movement in combination with the stepping out action (see Figure 4.1 frames 3-4, and Figure 4.2 frames 5-6).

- Turn the hips fully in the new direction while still maintaining the head and shoulders facing forward. This enables you to watch the play action and to fool your opponent when you step out laterally (see Figure 4.1 frames 6-7).

- Run in the sideward direction and then reverse directions again, if needed, without turning your shoulders. Think of yourself as having "swivel hips." This requires exceptional flexibility.

- The cut to your right (Figures 4.1-4.4) is executed in exactly the same manner as a cut to your left (Figures 4.6-4.7).

- Gradually increase your approach speed and speed of execution.

It is possible to see many variations of this basic technique. The differences are usually not critical as long as the key elements are executed. For example, it is not uncommon to see some players actually leap before planting the stopping leg. As soon as the stopping leg hits, the other leg is free to step out in a new direction. This is partially seen in Figure 4.1, frames 2 and 3. When the support leg is planted, if the body is stationary and the swing leg is off the ground, it is still an effective method of executing the cut.

Quickness is enhanced if you do not take any superfluous steps on executing the cut. If, from a running or walking stride you simply stick the leg hard and push off in the opposite direction, you will be faster than the person who must take two or more steps to execute the stop and then push-off. For example, it is common to see players us two steps to stop their forward motion. They first stop partially on the inside leg and then stop completely on the outside leg in order to execute the cut in the new direction (see Figures 4.3-4.4). In some cases a player may do a cross-over or partial cross-over step with the legs which also slows down the cutting action greatly (see Figure 4.4 frames 3-4).

90-Degree Cut to One Side from Forward Movement

Being able to execute a sharp 90-degree cut to one side from forward movement is also important for getting away from your opponent. The sharper and faster that you can make the cut the better are your chances of getting free to receive the ball or to execute a pass or kick. If you are on defense, if your opponent is able to execute quick cuts you will be able to keep up with her and as a result nullify her potential danger.

However, execution of a sharp cut is fairly difficult. You must have very good leg strength, explosive strength, excellent technique, and the flexibility needed to execute the cut as effectively as possible. Only in this way will you be able to execute the cut so that your opponent cannot anticipate your move so that you can get free. If on defense, this ability is the key to nullifying your opponent's effectiveness.

EXECUTION AND LEARNING PROGRESSION
- From a slow jog or walk, moving directly forward, plant your forward stride leg at a 45-90-degree angle to your path of movement, opposite the direction in which you wish to run. For example, for a cut to your right while moving directly forward, plant your left leg out to the left making contact on the inner side of the left foot (see Figure 4.8).
- As you forcefully stick the leg with the sole of the foot perpendicular to the intended direction of movement, lower your body weight while keeping your upper body facing forward (see Figure 4.8, frame 4 and Figure 4.9, frame 4). Begin to turn your hips

CUTTING ACTION (figures 4-8)

Figure 4.8-1

Figure 4.8-2

Figure 4.8-3

Figure 4.8-4

Figure 4.8-5

Figure 4.8-6

Figure 4.8-7

Figure 4.8-8

Figure 4.8-9

in the direction of the intended movement. Note that the players in Figures 4.8 and 4.9 turn the upper body and their heads rather than only the hips. As a result, the opponent can tell a change of direction is coming.

• As your body is lowered and your weight moves on to the left support leg, simultaneously raise the inside right leg (see Figures 4.8, frames 4-6 and 4.9, frames 4-5).

• Begin to push off with the left leg. Note that the stronger the initial eccentric contraction the faster you can stop and the sooner you can begin the push off. At the same time you turn the hips in the new direction of movement (see Figures 4.8 and 4.9, frames 5 and 6).

• As you conclude the push-off by fully extending the leg, step out with the free inside right leg, finish turning your upper body to the right and take a short running stride with your lower body fully facing the new direction of movement (see Figures 4.8 and 4.9, frames 5-7). If you have the necessary flexibility and strength, keep the head and shoulders facing forward while the hips and legs face the new direction as you run to the right. The exact

CUTTING ACTION (figures 4-9)

Figure 4.9-1   Figure 4.9-2   Figure 4.9-3   Figure 4.9-4

Figure 4.9-5   Figure 4.9-6   Figure 4.9-7

actions depend on your abilities and what you want to accomplish.

- Continue to accelerate as you prepare to execute another action or run until another change in direction is called for.

- As you master the approach and cut, gradually increase the speed of your approach and the cutting action.

- Keep working on technique and improving your physical abilities.

- The cut to your left is executed in the same manner as a cut to your right (see Figure 4.10 for basically the same execution).

45-Degree Angled Cut from Forward Movement

This cut is basically the same as the sharp 90-degree cut to one side from a forward moving direction. The main difference is that instead of making a sharp 90-degree cut to the right or left, you make approximately a 45-degree cut to the right or left and still keep running forward. The exact angle of cut depends on your speed and the purpose of the change in direction. It can vary from 10- to 80- degrees (see Figures 4.11 and 4.12).

CUTTING ACTION (figures 4-10)

| Figure 4.10-1 | Figure 4.10-2 | Figure 4.10-3 | Figure 4.10-4 |

| Figure 4.10-5 | Figure 4.10-6 | Figure 4.10-7 | Figure 4.10-8 |

CUTTING ACTION (figures 4-11)

| Figure 4.11-1 | Figure 4.11-2 | Figure 4.11-3 | Figure 4.11-4 |

| Figure 4.11-5 | Figure 4.11-6 | Figure 4.11-7 | Figure 4.11-8 |

The 45-degree angle cut is typically executed when you are running at higher speeds and want to go by your opponent for a shot, or to get free to receive a pass. You should be confident in your speed and cutting actions to carry you past your opponent. Even if your opponent is equally quick, you should still be able to get ahead of her by one or two steps. The key is to be close to your opponent when making the cut. If you cannot get by your opponent, check your execution for flaws.

EXECUTION AND LEARNING PROGRESSION

- From an easy run, stick your forward stride foot in front and out to the side about one to three feet to the side opposite your cutting direction, i.e., plant to the left to cut right (see Figures 4.11 and 4.12). The plant should be in front or slightly to the outside of your opponent.

- Lower your body weight on to the plant leg and turn the hips in the new direction so that your lower body momentum slows down but your upper body continues to move forward and to the side at the same speed in reaction to the opposite side foot plant. The inside leg should be off the ground (see Figure 4.11 frames 3-5).

CUTTING ACTION (figures 4-12)

Figure 4.12-1

Figure 4.12-2

Figure 4.12-3

Figure 4.12-4

Figure 4.12-5

Figure 4.12-6

- Keep your upper body moving forward and your head and shoulders facing front as you push-off.
- Push-off with the support leg and step out with the free leg at a 45 or so degree angle forward and to the side (see Figure 4.11, frames 5 and 6).
- Plant the free leg in a forward-side direction as you reassume the running stride (see Figures 4.11 frames 6-7, and 4.12 frames 5-6).
- Gradually increase speed of execution as your abilities improve.

Running Forward and then Changing Direction to Run Backward

In Figure 4.13, execution of this cut is basically the same as previously described. Only the approach and change of direction are different.

To change your forward run to a backward run, take a long forward step and turn the stopping leg and hips so that foot contact is on the inner sole of the foot to give you a good stopping surface (see Figure 4.13, frames 2-3).

EXECUTION AND LEARNING PROGRESSION
- Keep the head and shoulders in place as you stick the leg and lower your body. Free the other leg and let it swing inward (see Figure 4.13, frame 3). Note that the player maintains a basically forward shoulder facing position.
- Be sure that you turn the plant leg sufficiently to be able to touch down on the whole inside of the foot (see Figure 4.13 frame 3).
- If the right foot makes contact with the ground to stop, turn the hips to the left. If the left foot makes contact turn the hips to the right.

CUTTING ACTION (figures 4-13)

Figure 4.13-1

Figure 4.13-2

Figure 4.13-3

Figure 4.13-4

Figure 4.13-5

Figure 4.13-6

- When done correctly, it will appear as though you are leaning backward with the upper body, but you do not. This appearance is due to the lowered body position, forward plant of the leg and holding the head and shoulders in place. Do not purposely lean to the rear as it will increase your chances of slipping.

- Continue turning the hips and begin to push-off with the support leg and step out with the free leg (see Figure 4.13 frames 3-4).

- As you push-off, step out in the opposite direction with the rear, now forward, leg and complete turning the hips into the new direction. Begin to run to the rear in a regular running stride (see Figure 4.13 frames 5-6).

NOTE: You can keep looking in a forward direction as you run backwards, but only if you have sufficient flexibility in the midsection. In essence, you run backwards with the legs and hips facing backwards while still keeping your head and shoulders looking forward. In other words you run backward while looking forward. If you do not have the necessary midsection flexibility, then you must run with a crossover step or use a backpedaling action, both which are slower. When time is not critical, these latter two methods are acceptable. However, when time and speed of play do not allow the luxury of using these methods, you should work to be able to turn your lower body to run in one direction while keeping your head and shoulders facing in the opposite direction.

Some coaches advocate backpedaling, so that you can see what is happening in front. At times this action is needed, however for speed it is more effective to have the hips facing in the same direction as the run while you look in the opposite direction. This skill is essential for versatile players and can be done if you have sufficient flexibility in the midsection. You must be able to rotate the head and shoulders a full 90-degrees or more while the hips (and legs) remain facing in the opposite direction or vice versa. Such flexibility is critical for a soccer player, who must fall back quickly on defense while still looking at what her opponents are doing and the play action.

Running Backward and then Forward Changing Direction

In order to change directions from a backward run to a forward run, you must execute basically the same actions as when you are running forwards and change to running backwards. To execute the change in direction, you must stop your running backward, turn your hips and your legs to the front running position and run back in the direction from which you are came (see Figure 4.14).

EXECUTION AND LEARNING PROGRESSION

- From an easy run, take a long last step and forcefully stick the forward leg directly in front after turning the stopping leg and hips approximately 90 degrees. Turn the leg and hips to the opposite side of the forward stopping leg but keep your shoulders in place or lean the head and shoulders slightly away from the support leg (in the new direction) if your stopping stride is short (see Figure 4.14 frames 2-3).

- Land on the inside of the foot sole and then the whole foot as you lower the hips in the long last stride. At the same time, pick up the other leg so that it is free to step out (see Figure 4.14 frame 3).

- Step out with the free leg and push off with the rear leg forcefully. As you do this turn the hips and shoulders to the full front facing position. Move out as needed (see Figure 4.14 frames 4-6).

- Gradually increase your approach speed and speed of execution.

CUTTING ACTION (figures 4-14)

Figure 4.14-1

Figure 4.14-2

Figure 4.14-3

Figure 4.14-4

Figure 4.14-5

Figure 4.14-6

SELECTING THE CUTTING LEG

All cutting actions should be done on the outside leg. This means the leg which is planted opposite the direction into which you want to go. Thus if you are going to cut right while moving forward, stop and push off with the left leg and turn to your right. If you are going to cut to the left, stop your forward momentum and push off with the right leg and turn to your left. When making a change in direction to go left while moving sideways to the right, stop your side motion and push off with the right leg and turn to the left as you change directions. Push off with the right leg to go to the left when running sideways to the right and push off with the left leg to go to the right when running sideways to the left.

To make a change in direction when moving forward or backward, stop and push-off with whichever leg takes the last stride before you execute the cutting action. Thus if you stop and push-off with the right leg, you should turn to your left and if you stop and push-off with the left leg you should turn to the right. If you must turn in a particular direction, as for example, when keeping your eye on the action, you may have to take an extra step to insure that you turn in the same direction to stay with your opponent or to keep your eye on the action.

You should not push-off with the leg on the same side as your cutting direction, ie. cut with the right leg to go right or left leg to go left, except on rare occasions. This may happen in a situation where your opponent is blocking your pathway and it is imperative that you go around her. In this case, you must make the cut on whichever leg is out in front. For example, if you wish to go to the right and you execute the cutting action off the right leg, not only will it be executed slower, but it will never be as sharp as when you do it off the left leg. In addition, when you execute the change in direction off the inside leg you must do a leg crossover which puts you in an awkward position to make other last minute changes.

It is also important to understand that because of the reverse side ankle action in a cut off the inside leg, it may cause an ankle injury especially on a sharp cut. When executing a cut on the outside leg, and especially a sharp cut, there is 45-60 degrees of adduction (bend) in the subtalar joint of the ankle, i.e., when the foot is flat on the ground, the shin is angled between 45-60 degrees to the inside during the cut which is very safe. This is why you may lose your shoe if it was not tied all the way around the foot. It explains why many soccer (and football) players lose their low-top shoes during play. In an outside leg cutting action, you undergo adduction of the foot which greatly stretches the abductor muscles and tendons on the outside of the ankle. Because of this, they should be very strong.

If you execute the cut with the inside leg, instead of adduction occurring, you then have abduction which does not have the same range of motion in comparison to a cut off the outside leg. This limits your ability to make a sharp cut. If you attempted to execute a cut as sharp as with the outside leg, the stress placed on the ankle will be quite severe and may over-stretch the ligaments and tendons resulting in a painful "ankle sprain." A sprain on the inside ankle is usually much more severe than a sprain on the outside of the ankle. Because of this, as well as for greater speed of execution, it is important that you always execute the cut on the outside leg.

In spite of the ineffectiveness of a cut to the same side as the cutting leg, many athletes still use this inside leg action. I strongly recommend that you check to see if you are one of these athletes and then make the necessary changes. Not only will it help to prevent injury but you will then be much quicker and sharper in your direction changes. Always make the change in direction off the outside leg. The only time you may have to push-off with the inside leg is when you have to cut immediately on a signal or some action by your opponent. Such instances should be rare. When you push-off with the outside leg, not only will you be able to get away from your opponent quicker to get into the clear, but you will also be better able to keep up with your opponent when she makes quick changes in direction.

SUMMARY AND OTHER IMPORTANT DETAILS

- Be sure to keep your head and shoulders in place as you plant ("stick") the leg to stop lower body movement so that your opponent will not be able to read your next move (see Figure 4.10, frame 4). There should be no side lean as exhibited by the player in Figure 4.10.

- Do not lean over or away from your stopping leg. This costs valuable time. Keep your trunk erect (see Figures 4.1, 4.4, 4.8, 4.12).

- Your stopping leg should be out to the side and/or in front of your body (in relation to your new intended line of movement) with your upper body remaining in position (see Figures 4.1 to 4.4 and 4.6 to 4.12). Use only your lower body in the cutting action.

- The plant leg should not only stop your body forward motion, but cushion some of the braking forces and at the same time, generate sufficient force that can be returned to push you in the opposite direction. The faster and more forcefully you stop your forward motion, the greater the accumulation of energy to prepare the muscles to contract explosively to push you in the new direction.

- Push-off forcefully and step out with the inside free leg (see Figures 4.1, 4.6, and 4.8).

- Continue turning your body so that you now face the opposite direction (or the new intended direction) and have returned to your running stride.

- Essentially you must execute five actions at one time:
  - "Stick" the forward leg to stop your forward motion.
  - Lower your weight, keeping the head and shoulders back.
  - Turn your hips toward the new direction.
  - Push-off with the support leg.
  - Step out with the swing leg in the new running stride.

It must be stressed that all of the above actions are accomplished in one step. That's right, one step! This is why technique of executing a cut is so important in increasing your quickness and your ability to elude, (or to stay with) your opponent. All too often, girls (especially younger girls) take two or three short stutter steps to stop their movement in one direction before stepping out in the new direction. Or they execute a partial stop on one leg and then a full stop on the other leg (see Figures 4.3 and 4.4). Doing this loses valuable seconds. In addition, your opponent then knows that a change in direction is coming and can prepare herself to do likewise and keep up with you as you make the cut.

The importance of agility for soccer players can be illustrated by Melissa, a young athlete with whom I had worked for several years. She was also a cross country runner on the high school track team and was a regional champion. She was great when it came to running straight line distances but could not execute cutting actions.

I worked on her cutting actions for several weeks until they became automatic. She then played in a game against collegiate players even though she did not have any prior college experience. During play she made such sharp changes in direction, that she was able to get clear of all opponents and get every pass for a shot or other play. Her more experienced opponents were amazed at her ability to elude them. The same can happen to you. The key is to learn how to execute the cuts and to improve your physical abilities related to these movements with specialized strength and explosive exercises.

See Chapter 8 for corrections on cutting techniques.

5

Specialized Strength Exercises for Running and Cutting

Specialized strength exercises, based on biomechanical and kinesiological analyses of effective running and cutting, mimic the key actions in these skills. The exercises duplicate not only the exact movements involved but also the range of motion and type of muscular contraction that occurs. In the initial stages of training, the exercises may not duplicate the exact muscular contraction since it is often necessary to first prepare the muscles to be able to do some of these exercises especially in an explosive manner. Because of this, some of the exercises are done at different speeds or with slight modifications before duplicating the exact conditions seen in explosive running for short distances or in explosive cutting actions. By doing specialized strength exercises you will see immediate improvement in your running and cutting.

To select the exercises most beneficial for you, determine the lagging aspects of your technique as well as the physical abilities that you are lacking. Your training program should reflect these aspects so that you can bring up the lagging areas and make them commensurate with your strong points. You must also improve your strong points, especially if they are key joint movements. Thus, a biomechanical and kinesiological analysis of your running and cutting is important to becoming the best player possible.

If you participate in a general conditioning program, you may see some improvement in your running and cutting, especially if you were in poor shape when you started. But, if the strength and other exercises do not duplicate what you do in running or cutting, or if the exercises do not enhance your strong or improve your weak points, you will not see all the improvement that is possible. General physical preparation, however, can serve as a strong base for doing special exercises.

To strengthen the muscles as needed in running and cutting, it is necessary to do a multitude of different exercises, especially when first starting. You must involve all the major and minor muscles in many different exercises so that the entire body is involved. Strengthening only the major muscles and ignoring some of the relatively minor muscles, especially of the foot and ankle often leads to injury. Keep in mind that you are only as strong as your weakest link.

To greatly improve your running and cutting, you must strengthen the muscles as they function in the key joint actions. This means you should do at least one strength exercise for each major joint action involved. Use different speeds of execution to accustom the muscles to changes in running speed and quickness of cutting movements.

You should do exercises to improve your technique as well as your physical qualities. Since the key actions in running and cutting involve not only the agonist (main) but the antagonistic (opposing) muscles, you should do exercises for each set of muscles and often in all three muscle contraction regimes. In this way, you strengthen the muscles on both sides of the joint in all their actions to duplicate what occurs in running and cutting and at the same time help to prevent injury.

One of the most neglected areas in a typical soccer weight training program is the foot. The foot is composed of not only many bones but also many muscles, ligaments and tendons that are needed to keep the foot in good position so that it can carry out its many functions. For example, the foot dictates what happens above the feet, i.e., in the knee, hip and even lower backs. The foot is in almost constant contact with the ground and must be positioned in many different ways when contact with the ball is made Because of this, it must be able to handle the hitting (kicking) forces in addition to those experienced in running and cutting. Maintaining a good arch in the foot is crucial to not only shock absorption when the foot lands on the ground but also in all cutting and push-off actions.

The benefits of stronger feet from a health and sports performance perspective has been documented many times over. A structurally sound foot is capable of naturally controlling impact forces through the energy storage mechanisms (mainly the ligaments and tendons) that are inherent in the muscle-joint make-up. In addition a structurally sound foot provides the body with a stable base of support when running over diversified terrain and when cutting on uneven ground. Stronger feet promote improved body alignment, better energy transfer, decrease susceptibility to overuse injuries and improve your dynamic stabilization abilities.

Since the foot plays many roles in soccer, strengthening the muscles of the foot (and ankle) is needed not only for the prevention of injury but for enhancing performance. For example, when you land on the ball of the foot or mid-foot, the muscles and tendons of the foot arch are the first to come into play. They undergo a quick forceful stretch and gain tension for initial shock absorption. They then undergo even greater tension and, as a result, accumulate energy, which is then given back in the push-off. This is a very important role of the foot! Do not rely on shoes to do this for you.

Because of the importance of the feet, it is surprising that strength exercises for the foot are rarely recommended for soccer players. This may be due to the belief that soccer shoes can duplicate or enhance the functions of the foot. In reality, the shoes do not come close to doing this, and in many cases they actually interfere with the proper functioning of the foot and leg muscles and tendons.

For example, according to some researchers, running shoes lead to foot, ankle, knee, and hip problems instead of preventing them. (Similar data is not available for soccer shoes.) Researchers have even found that the number of running injuries increases with the price of the running shoes! Rather than relying on running shoes, you should strengthen the foot muscles, tendons, and ligaments so the feet and legs can perform their normal functions more effectively than any shoe. And, you should wear shoes that allow your feet to function normally.

Many of the muscles that perform an action at the ankle also play a very important role in the foot. For example, the tibialis anterior muscle, located on the front of the shin, helps stabilize the inside of the ankle and support the foot arch. In addition, it is the key muscle to prevent shin splints.

Since most of the muscles of the foot are relatively small and the muscles that move the foot at the ankle are relatively long and thin, there is usually very little muscular development visible after these muscles are strengthened. Because of this there is a tendency by players to ignore these muscles since they like to see muscular changes from their weight training program.

In addition, many of these muscles take time to develop and to become sufficiently strong to see results in function. Because of this, players have a tendency to ignore doing exercises for the foot. Foot exercises also take somewhat longer to do in comparison to typical lower body exercises such as the squat or lunge. As a consequence, it forces you to persevere on a strengthening program. However the values of doing foot exercises far outweigh the negatives.

Some of the better exercises that should be done for the foot include the following:

Picking up marbles with the toes. Assume a seated position with a bunch of marbles spread out on the floor in front of the chair. Put your bare foot on top of the marbles and pick up as many as possible with the toes. Hold the marbles in the toes and then raise the leg and bring the foot inward to place the marbles in your opposite hand. When you execute toe flexion to grab the marbles, you work the muscles on the underside of the foot, especially the muscles of the arch. By bringing the foot up and turning the sole of the foot inward to put the marbles in the opposite hand, you work the tibialis anterior which also supports the arch. If marbles are not available, you can put your foot on a towel on the floor and then grasp the towel with the toes, pulling in repetitively as much as possible.

Barefoot walking. When you walk barefoot, the toes will automatically flex on each step which in turn builds up the arch of the foot. In addition, every time you put weight on the foot, the muscles of the foot sole must work to support the arch. As a result, barefoot walking strengthens the entire underside of the foot. Walking in sand is even more effective because of the non-stable surface.

Walking on the balls of the feet when barefooted. When you walk only on the balls of the feet, the muscles on the underside of the foot automatically contract to hold the foot stable to allow you to walk in this position. Initially, begin walking for very short distances, and then gradually increase the amount so that you can go longer.

Jogging in bare feet. Jogging with the landing occurring on the balls of the feet is also extremely effective for strengthening the underside of the foot, especially the muscles, ligaments and tendons of the arch. Be sure to start off slowly and to gradually increase the distance covered.

Barefoot running. Run barefoot only after you have done the above exercises and feel that your feet are now capable of withstanding the stresses involved. When you run barefooted, you will have to use good technique. It is very difficult, if not impossible, to land on the heel of the foot because of the pain you will experience. Be sure to land more on the ball or whole foot so that the underside of the foot automatically goes to work to support the body and to slightly cushion the landing. In addition, the tendons will gain energy which will then be given back in the push-off.

Barefoot Science

Because it is sometimes impossible to walk or run when barefooted, you can still develop greater strength of the foot arch muscles by using insoles made by Barefoot Science. The insoles have inserts that are placed on the insoles dome contour directly underneath the arch of the foot as it sits within the shoe. The inserts range from relatively soft to much firmer so that they provide a stimulus to the bottom of the foot. As a result, you activate the body proprioceptive mechanisms which initiates contraction of the muscles in the foot and to a certain extent, the lower leg. By using progressively firmer inserts, the foot arch muscles continually get stronger while wearing your soccer or everyday shoes. This is a simple but effective way of increasing the strength of the arch which plays such an important role not only in foot health but in soccer running and cutting. And the strengthening takes place while going about your everyday activities and while you are playing!

The exercises that follow have been created from biomechanical and kinesiological analyses of world class soccer players, runners and great open field runners who execute quick and powerful cutting actions when changing directions while running. The exercises have been used for many years and have proven both their safety and effectiveness. If you feel any major discomfort in executing these exercises be sure to check on how you are doing the exercise or if you have any physical problems that do not allow you to do them as needed. It is important that you execute the exercises as described to get their full benefits and to prevent injury.

Execution with rubber tubing is preferred if you work out by yourself at home or at the neighborhood field. If you work out in a gym, execution on specialized pieces of equipment may be more appropriate for some exercises as may be the use of free weights. In general, machine exercises are not recommended because they do not involve balance and are often too constricted in the movement pathways allowed. In addition, all machines do not produce the same effects because of differences in their leverage and/or pulley arrangements. Thus, if you are going to use machines in the gym, be sure that they can be adjusted for your body and that you receive directions on how they should be used. It seems every company makes the machines slightly different and therefore it requires a certain learning curve in order to use the machine effectively. This includes not only standard machines but also free-weight machines, such as the lat pull-down and leg extension.

Heel Raises (figures 5-1)

Figure 5.1-a   Figure 5.1-b

SPECIALIZED STRENGTH AND FLEXIBILITY EXERCISES

Heel Raises

This exercise is needed to strengthen the muscles involved in ankle joint extension – the key joint action in the push-off in running and to a good extent in cutting.

Execution with Rubbing Tubing.

Stand on a stable board 2-4" in height on the balls of the feet so that heels are free to move. Secure the middle of the rubber tubing around and under the balls of your feet or under the platform or attachment board you are standing on. Then attach the ends of the tubing to a non-slip belt (as in the Active Cords set) fastened around the waist or to the handles which are then held in the hands at shoulder height. Be sure that there is adequate tension in the tubing when first starting.

When you are ready, keep the legs straight and lower the heels until you feel a stretch in the Achilles' tendon. Then rise up as high as possible and hold for one to two seconds (see Figure 5.1 a,.b.). Lower the heels and then repeat going through a full range of motion on each repetition. If you have difficulty balancing yourself, hold on to a stationary object. Also, if you use a short board, have another player hold down the far edge as in Figure 5.1.

To develop some of the assistive muscles and to bring in other foot actions, you should change foot positions. For example, point your toes inward and then rise up for greater strengthening of the tibialis anterior.

Toe Raises (figures 5-2)

Figure 5.2-a   Figure 5.2-b

Position your toes outward and then do the exercise to involve the peroneal muscles and the extensor digitorum longus located on the lateral sides of the shins. Always keep the feet hip-width apart during execution and the legs fully extended.

Execution in the Gym

There are now various standing and seated heel raise machines available in gyms. Both versions are good although some players experienced discomfort on certain machines but can do the exercise well on others. Because of this, you should check what is available in your gym and find a machine that can be used safely and effectively by you. If not, stay with the exercise described above with rubber tubing.

When you do the heel raise exercise in a gym, there are certain key elements that you must adhere to regardless of the machine in use. This means that you should keep the legs straight at all times when you extend the ankle joints. Also, try to maintain your body in a straight line from the feet through the trunk so that it can more closely duplicate your body position when running and cutting.

Toe Raises

The purpose of this exercise is to duplicate the raising of the front part of the foot as occurs during the forward swing of the shin in running and cutting and to help prevent shin splints. The toe raise is also needed to balance the calf muscle development and so that you can develop even greater strength of the muscles. The more you strengthen the calf and shin muscles, the more development you can get of either one.

Execution with Rubber Tubing

Assume a seated position on the floor with the leg to be exercised extended and with one end of the Active Cord attached to the ball of the foot area. The other end should be secured at the same height and there should be tension on the cord at all times. Point the toes as far as possible away from yourself and then pull the toe-ball area of the foot back toward the shin as far as possible (see Figures 5.2 a, b). Hold for one or two seconds in the up position and then relax and return to the original position before repeating. Note that you cannot raise the foot much above the anatomical (neutral) position. Thus it is important that you go through the maximal range of motion beginning with the extended ankle position.

Execution in the Gym

If you work out in a gym, the toe raise exercise is best done on a Tib Exerciser machine. Other devices are also available so you should check with your gym to see what they have and how you should use it. Regardless of the equipment you use, most important is that the toe area of the feet be placed under the resistance rollers with the feet extended maximally before you raise the toe portion of the feet as high as possible and hold for one-two seconds before lowering.

Knee (Leg) Extensions (figures 5-3)

Figure 5.3-a

Figure 5.3-b

Knee (Leg) Extensions

This exercise strengthens the quadriceps muscle especially the vastus lateralis and medialis muscles of the quadriceps femoris muscle group. These muscles play a major role in keeping the patella in its groove to prevent some of the more common knee problems. Knee extensions also play a role in swinging the shin out when running and cutting.

Execution with Rubber Tubing

Assume a standing position with one end of the Active Cord attached to an ankle strap on the leg to be exercised and the other end attached at knee or below-knee height. Stand with your back facing the non-movable attachment and position yourself far enough away so that there is some tension on the tubing. When you are ready, hold yourself erect or support yourself on a stationary object or put your hand on an assistant for stability.

Bring the thigh up to about a 45-degree angle with the shin folded underneath. Hold the thigh in place and swing the shin out (knee joint extension) until the leg is straight. Return to the initial position and repeat (see Figure 5.3 a,b). There may be slight movement of the thigh upward or downward as you completely extend the leg. This natural movement is an important safety factor. It makes the exercise safer and more effective than immobilizing the thigh as in the typical leg extension exercise in the gym.

Execution in the Gym

The most common exercise in the gym is the seated leg extension on a leg extension machine. This can be an effective exercise but it also has an element of danger because of the stationary thigh. During execution, great pressure is built up in the knee as the leg is extended especially when there is great resistance. As a result, it can cause injury. Because of this, I recommend use of a low cable pulley or rubber tubing. Execution on a low pulley cable is basically the same as with the Active Cords.

If you do the leg extension exercise on a leg extension machine, go through only half the range of motion. Begin with the knee at a 45-60 degree angle and then extend the leg until it is straight. Return to the 45-60 degree angle and then repeat. To target the vastus lateralis and medialis, you must fully extend the leg, but because of the pressure built up, do not use extremely heavy resistance. Do more repetitions rather than fewer repetitions to prevent the possibility of injury.

Standing Leg Curl (figures 5-4)

Figure 5.4-a

Figure 5.4-b

Standing Leg Curl

Increased hamstring muscle strength helps to stabilize the knee and to prevent lower thigh hamstring injuries. It can also be used to correct excessive inward or outward rotation of the feet.

Execution with Rubber Tubing

Assume a standing position with one leg raised 45-60 degrees horizontal and one end of the Active Cord attached to the ankle strap. The free end of the cord should be secured about knee high. When ready, hold the thigh in place as you bend the knee to bring the shin under the thigh. Return to the initial position and repeat (see Figure 5.4 a,b).

Execution in the Gym

There are several different types of machines that can be used to do the knee curl in the gym. They include a standing version, two lying face-down versions, and a seated version. Of the three, the seated version is preferred as it gives you a stronger contraction of the hamstrings. If you use the face-down lying version, use the angled bench so that the hips are placed higher to make the exercise more effective when you bend the knees. In the standing version, you work one leg at a time so that you can concentrate on what is happening with the muscles. Regardless of which machine you use, be sure that the knees are free of support and that the back of your lower shins rest against the underside of the resistance rollers. Bend your knees until the angle in the knee joint is 90-degrees or less (measured from the back of the thigh to the back of the shin).

The Squat (figures 5-5)

Figure 5.5-a

Figure 5.5-b

The Squat

This exercise is needed to strengthen the anterior thigh (quadriceps) muscles to prevent excessive up and down movements during the landing and support phase in running, when changing directions in running, in the running start and in the push-off when stepping out. In addition, the squat is one of the best exercises for the prevention of knee problems.

Execution with Rubber Tubing

Place the middle of the Active Cord under both feet and hold the handles attached to the ends in the hands on extended arms. If greater tension is needed, stand with the hands up alongside the shoulders with the elbows pointed downward. When in a standing position, there should be strong tension on the cords. Stand with your feet approximately hip width apart with your toes pointed straight ahead or turned out slightly.

Inhale and hold your breath as you flex your knees and lower your body into the squat position keeping the heels in contact with the ground and the lower back in its normal (slightly arched) curvature. Your knees should come forward slightly and your buttocks should move to the rear and then straight down. The trunk should incline forward up to 45 degrees from the vertical in the down position. Be sure to maintain the slight arch in the lower back at all times (see Figure 5.5 a,b).

After reaching the bottom position, reverse directions by forcefully extending the legs and rise up. Exhale when you pass the most difficult portion of the up phase, or as you approach the full standing position. Keep your eyes focused directly in front. The bottom position is determined by your ability to hold the arch in the lower back. If your spine begins to round in the down position, you should stop your descent immediately. The point at which the back rounding occurs determines how far you lower the body up to the thigh level position.

Execution in the Gym

There are many different machines and variants of the squat that can be done in the gym. In regard to machines, there is a Smith machine, a Hack machine and some forms of leg press machines that can duplicate the squat action. For example, the lying leg press is analogous to the Smith machine or Hack squat which are done in a vertical standing position. The squat can also be done with free weights holding dumbbells in the hand or with a barbell on the shoulder. When you begin using heavy weights, then the squat should be done in a power rack for greater safety.

When using machines such as the Smith or Hack squat, it is important that you place the feet out in front of the body so that when you go into the squat, the trunk will remain erect and you will not have excessive flexion in the knees nor will the knees go beyond your base of support. When you are in the down position, especially with heavy weights, the knees should be directly above the toe area of the feet. The further out in front that the knees go, the more dangerous it is to the knee joints.

When doing the lying leg press or incline leg press, be sure that you do not bring the knees too close to the chest. Doing so rounds the lower back and may be injurious. The key in all cases, is to go to the point where there is a 90-degree angle in the knee joint and then reverse directions and extend the legs. Keep in mind that in soccer play and in running and cutting a very deep squat is not called for. Forty-five to ninety degrees is the maximum that is typically seen in the course of play.

Execution Variant – Delay Squat

The delay squat is a very effective exercise for increasing your eccentric and isometric strength, in addition to concentric strength. It also helps to develop an explosive contraction when you reach maximum tension in the muscle. To execute, do the squat exercise as indicated above except for the following changes: Lower the body very, very slowly for a count of 4 (approximately 4 seconds). In this period of time you should lower your body approximately 4-6 inches. After the count of 4, you hold the position for another count of 4 (approximately 4 seconds in the isometric regime). You then again lower the body very slowly for

The Lunge (figures 5-6)

Figure 5.6-a

Figure 5.6-b

Figure 5.6-c

Figure 5.6-d

another count of 4 followed by a hold for a count of 4, and then repeat again for a total of three repetitions. After you hold the down position, come up as quickly as possible trying to jump as forcefully as you can. Because of the resistance (and muscle fatigue), you will be unable to leave the floor but you will develop some explosiveness of the muscle at maximum tension.

The Lunge

This exercise is needed to actively stretch the hip flexors and to strengthen the quadriceps and hamstring muscles. In addition, the lunge is a very important exercise in cutting actions and for getting low. It gives you the flexibility and strength that you need to take a long low step when reaching for the ball and to get the body low when changing directions.

Execution with Rubber Tubing

Secure the Active Cords belt around the hips and attach the rubber tubing onto one of the hooks in the middle of the back of the hips. The stationary attachment should be approximately knee-to-hip high. Assume a standing position and when you are ready, inhale and hold your breath as you step forward with a very long stride keeping your trunk in a vertical position. Upon landing, hold the vertical trunk position and then slowly lower the upper body straight down. In the bottom position you should have approximately 90 degrees of flexion in your forward leg and most of your weight should be on it. Your rear leg should remain straight but relaxed (see Figure 5.6 a,b).

After reaching the down position you should feel muscle tension in your front leg quadriceps muscle and lower back erector spinae muscles together with a strong stretch of the hip flexors of the rear leg. After holding the lowermost position for one-two seconds, push-off with the forward leg to shift the weight backward. Take a step or two to return to the original position. The pull of the cords assist on the return. Exhale and repeat the exercise stepping out with the other leg.

Execution in the Gym

When you do the lunge with rubber tubing, emphasis is on the stepping out and lowering portion. Execution in the gym however, without the use of Active Cords, concentrates more on the up and down action. To be more specific to the actions in soccer, it is important that you do most of your lunges with Active Cords to work on the stepping out and lowering aspects.

In the gym, the lunge is typically done with dumbbells in the hand or with a barbell on the shoulders. Execution is the same as with the Active Cords. Note that you can also do the lunge with dumbbells on the field (see Figure 5.6 c,d).

Also effective is to rise up with the forward leg in place after each lunge (known as a walking lunge). This action strengthens the hip extensor muscles as does execution with the Active Cords. When you have developed sufficient hip joint flexibility the knee of your rear-leg should almost touch the floor in the bottom position when the leg is kept straight.

Forward Knee Drive (figures 5-7)

Figure 5.7-a

Figure 5.7-b

Forward Knee Drive

This exercise is needed to duplicate the action of driving the thigh forward in the running stride and after executing a cut. It is also important when taking a quick first step.

Execution with Rubber Tubing

Attach one end of the Active Cord to a stationary object about knee high and the other end to an ankle strap around the ankle. Stand far enough away from the attachment so that there is ample tension on the cord when the leg is behind the body. Stand erect and hold onto a stationary object to stabilize the upper body. When you are ready, drive the thigh forward vigorously and at the same time bend the knee so that the shin remains basically parallel to the ground during the forward drive. The thigh should stop when it is approximately 45-degrees forward (see Figure 5.7 a,b).

Do not drive the thigh upward. Maintain an erect body position during execution. Some forward lean may be necessary when starting in order to get the leg back, behind the body. For variety you can extend the support leg and rise up on the balls of the feet as the knee is driven forward.

Execution in the Gym

In order to duplicate the knee drive exercise in a gym, you must use a low pulley cable. If your gym has a moveable pulley attachment, set it

Pawback (figures 5-8)

Figure 5.8-a

Figure 5.8-b

approximately knee high so that you can execute the exercise the same way as with the Active Cords. Execution is exactly the same.

Pawback (Leg Pulldown)

This exercise is needed to improve the thigh pullback action which occurs in preparation for touchdown in running and when taking a long second step.

Execution with Rubber Tubing

Attach the Active Cord to a high or above the head stationary object and the other end to the ankle strap on the leg to be exercised. Stand back from the point of attachment so that the cord is at about a 45-degree angle when you raise the leg to a below parallel position. There should be tension on the cord. When you are ready, straighten the leg and pull down and back fairly vigorously. Contact on the ground should be on the whole foot or ball of the foot directly under the body or just slightly to the rear. Hold your body in an erect, stable position during execution (see Figure 5.8 a,b).

Execution in the Gym

This exercise can only be done with a pulley cable in the gym. Use a high pulley so that you can pull the leg down and back to work the hip extensor muscles. Execution is the same as with the Active Cords.

Glute-Ham Gastroc Raise

This is the only exercise that strengthens the hamstring muscles and their tendons at the hip joint and at the knee joint in sequence. The strength gained gives you more power in the pawback action in running. The glute-ham-gastroc raise has proven to be especially effective in prevention and rehabilitation of hamstring injuries. Runners who do this exercise regularly have rarely, if ever, experienced a hamstring injury.

Glute-Ham Gastroc Raise (figures 5-9)

Figure 5.9-a

Figure 5.9-b

Figure 5.9-c

Execution

This exercise is typically executed in the gym on the Yessis Back Machine, formerly known as the Glute-Ham Developer. It is described here because of its unique value in developing the hamstring and lower back muscles. To position yourself, assume a face down position so that support is on the upper thighs when your feet are placed between the rear rollers for support. When your legs are in place lower your trunk over and down the front side of the seat and hold the back in its normal curvature. Your upper body and pelvic girdle should form a straight line from the hip joint to the head (see Figure 5.9 a).

Inhale slightly more than usual and hold your breath as your raise your trunk with the axis in the hips. Your back should remain rigid in its slightly arched position. Raise your trunk until the body forms a straight line from your head to your feet (see Figure 5.9 b). Then keep the hip joint extensor muscles under contraction and bend your knees. Keep raising your straight body (from your knees to your head) to approximately a 30-degree angle above the horizontal (see Figure 5.9c).

Back Raise (figures 5-10)

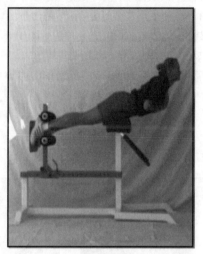

Figure 5.10-a   Figure 5.10-b

After reaching the top position, exhale and relax slightly but keep the lower back in its slightly arched position. Lower your body by straightening the legs and then flex at the hips to return to the original position. Execute the exercise at a moderate rate of speed.

Back Raise (Spinal Extension)

This exercise is needed to strengthen the lower back muscles in a very safe manner. It is the best exercise for strengthening the erector spinae muscle of the lower back through the full ROM. Strength of the lower back muscles enables you to maintain an erect trunk position while running and cutting and helps to prevent lower back injury. The back raise is most conveniently and safely done on a Yessis Back Machine or on a high sturdy table with an assistant to hold your legs down.

Execution

Adjust the setting so that when you position yourself face down over the curved seat of the Yessis Back Machine and your feet are placed between the rear pads, your entire pelvic girdle rests on the seat. Lower your upper body over the seat and relax the spinal muscles. In this position your spine will naturally assume a rounded position and will be at approximately a 60-degree angle below the horizontal (see Figure 5.10 a). Your legs should be fully extended and kept straight at all times.

From the down position, inhale slightly more than usual and hold your breath as you extend (straighten) your spine to raise the upper body

Reverse Back Raise (figures 5-11)

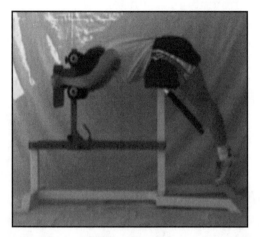
Figure 5.11-a

Figure 5.11-b

until it is slightly higher than your legs, i.e., so that there is a slight arch in the lower back (see Figure 5.10 b). After reaching the uppermost position hold for one or two seconds and then exhale and return to the original position under control. When you reach the lowermost position relax your muscles and then repeat.

If doing the exercise on a high sturdy table, be sure that someone holds your legs down firmly and that your pelvis is at the end of the table. Place a small towel on the edge of the table to create a little more pressure in the lower abdomen when you do the exercise. Your navel should be at the far edge of the table. Execute the same as on the Yessis Back Machine.

Reverse Back Raise

If you are uncomfortable when your trunk is in an upside-down position as in back raise exercise, do the reverse back raise. In this exercise, you position yourself in the opposite manner on the Yessis Back Machine or on a high sturdy table holding on to the sides.

Execution

The abdomen should be directly on top of the rounded seat (or at the end of the table) and your legs should hang down at approximately a 60-degree angle. Your hands should hold the back plate or rollers to stabilize the upper body (or sides of the table). When you are ready, inhale and raise the legs until they are above the level of the trunk, then exhale as you lower the legs and repeat (see Figure 5.11 a,b).

For greater resistance, add ankle weights or rubber tubing. To execute with Active Cords, place an attachment board under the front supports of the machine to secure it and attach both ends of the rubber tubing to the hook directly under the legs. Wrap the middle of the cord around both legs. There should be slight tension on the tubing when you are in the down position. When you are ready, inhale and hold your breath as you raise the leg(s) until they are slightly higher than the level of your back. Then exhale and return to the initial position. Relax for a moment and then repeat. Be sure to keep the legs straight during execution.

Good Morning (modified deadlift)

This pulling exercise is used mainly to stretch and strengthen the hamstring muscles and their upper tendons. It also improves isometric strength of the lower back muscles to hold the spine in place when executing various moves.

Execution

Stand erect with dumbbells in the hands held on extended arms. Your feet should be hip to shoulder width apart. The legs should be straight and the lumber spine should be in its normal alignment, i.e., with a slight arch at all times.

When you are ready, inhale slightly more than usual and hold your breath as you bend forward from the hip joints. Push your hips back-

Good Morning (figures 5-12)

Figure 5.12-a

Figure 5.12-b

ward as your trunk inclines forward and down to the horizontal position (or as far as your flexibility will allow). After reaching the lowermost position, reverse directions and rise up to the starting position. Exhale as you approach the upright position (see Figure 5.12 a,b). To increase the difficulty, hold the dumbbells shoulder level as you do the exercise.

This exercise can also be done with a barbell on the shoulders, but only if you are sufficiently strong. With more weight, there is greater stress placed on the lower back muscles which must be strong to hold the arched position.

Reverse Sit-up

This exercise is used to strengthen the lower section of the abdominals through a full range of motion. These muscles work to rotate the hips so that the hip flexors can drive the thigh forward more forcefully. Thus, this exercise is especially important for increasing speed because of the faster thigh drive in running. It also improves driving the thigh forward when taking the first step in a cutting action and to start running.

Reverse Sit up (figures 5-13)

| Figure 5.13-a | Figure 5.13-b | Figure 5.13-c |

Execution

Lie on your back with your arms alongside the body and your feet off the floor, knees bent and thighs vertical. This is the starting position. When you are ready, inhale slightly more than usual and then hold your breath as you rotate the pelvis up and toward the shoulders until your hips are off the floor. Keep your knees bent tightly as you do this exercise so that the action stresses the lower abdominals (see Figure 5.13 a,b).

Push down with hands to help raise your hips (and legs) and to en-sure adequate rotation of the pelvic girdle. In the ending position your knees should be about chest-high. Keep your head and shoulders re-laxed throughout the upward movement. Exhale as you return to the initial position, pause and then repeat.

When doing the exercise in this manner becomes easy, place your arms overhead so that they cannot assist in execution. Then do the exer-cise concentrating on only the lower abdominals to rotate the hips up-ward. To involve more of the upper portion of the abdominal muscles, continue rotating the pelvis and legs up and over until the knees are close to your head. This is a more advanced movement and one in which you get more active stretching of the lower back (see Figure 5.13 c).

CUTTING ACTIONS

Cutting actions involve some of the same leg and hip actions as used in running. Thus, some of the exercises that you do for improvement of running will also enhance your cutting ability. However, there are also many movements that are specific to cutting. The key special strength exercises for these movements, are as follows.

Leg Abduction

Leg (hip) abduction is the main action in stepping out to the side to plant the support (braking) leg as well as being the key action to initiate the push-off when driving the hips (body) in the new direction (see fig-ure 5.14). Since your weight is concentrated in the hips, when you put the hips in motion, it is the same as placing your body into motion. Note that the action in this exercise (figure 5.14) occurs in the hip joint and that the leg is in motion, not the hips as in Figure 5.15.

Execution

To execute, assume a standing position with one end of the Active Cords attached to the ankle strap around the lower leg to be in motion and the other end to a stationary object. Stand sideways with the leg to be exercised furthest from the attachment so that the cord goes across the other leg to its stationary attachment. Assume a well-balanced stand-ing position holding onto a stationary object or another player to main-tain the trunk (upper body) in place at all times.

When you are ready, inhale and hold your breath as you pull the leg out to the side as far as possible while keeping the trunk erect. After reaching the uppermost position, exhale and return to the initial posi-tion, pause and then repeat. As you pull the leg out to the side be sure to

Leg Abduction (figures 5-14)

| Figure 5.14-a | Figure 5.14-b |

keep the leg straight (or locked) and the toes pointed directly in front. Execution should be fairly vigorous in order to reach as high a position as possible while still keeping the upper body in place (see Figure 5.14 a,b).

Hip Abduction

To duplicate even more closely the action of driving the hips forward when pushing off in a cutting action, you should do the hip abduction exercise with the hips in motion. To effectively do this exercise, use Active Cords or a low pulley cable as found in the gym.

Execution

Secure the non-slip Active Cords belt around the hips with one end of the rubber tubing attached to the side of the hip belt and the other to an immovable object. When you are ready, keep the feet and shoulders in place and then drive the hips sideways. After you master this action, pick up the non-support (outside) leg and step out as you drive the hips (entire upper body) forward with a strong push off the inside (rear) leg. This will give you the feel of the push-off and driving the hips at the same time as you step out to the side (see Figure 5.15 a,b).

Hip Adduction

Although hip joint adduction is not a key movement in cutting, (except when you pull your leg across in an inside leg cut) it is important

Hip Abduction (figures 5-15)

Figure 5.15-a   Figure 5.15-b

that the adductor muscles be strong to balance the abductor muscles and to prevent groin injury. Increased strength of the adductors is also important in pulling the outside leg in when going into the side running pattern, in initiating the thigh drive in running and when stepping out. Execution is best done with Active Cords or a low pulley cable as found in a gym.

Execution

Stand with your feet apart with the inner leg to be exercised hooked to the rubber tubing at the ankle. The other end should be attached to an immovable object close to the ground. Hold onto a partner or a stationary object to hold the trunk erect during execution. When you are ready, shift your hips (weight) to the outside leg and then, keeping the leg to be exercised straight, pull it in to the other leg. Return to the initial position and repeat. Inhale and hold your breath as you pull the leg in and exhale as you return to the initial position. Be sure to keep the upper body erect so that there is no side leaning during the pull (see Figure 5.16 a,b).

The Side Lunge

The side lunge is one of the most important exercises for improving your cutting ability and for preventing groin injuries. By doing this exercise, you get additional flexibility in the hip joint by stretching and strengthening the adductor (groin) muscles, which are often injured in side movements. You also develop maximum ROM and the ability to

Hip Adduction (figures 5-16)

| Figure 5.16-a | Figure 5.16-b | Figure 5.16-c |

lower the body as needed when taking a long step out to the side. This exercise is an extension of the hip abduction exercise with the hips in motion (see figure 5-17).

Execution

Secure the Active Cords belt around the hips with one end of the rubber tubing attached to the side of the hip and the other to an immovable object. When you are ready, keep the upper body erect and drive the hips sideways. Pick up the outside leg and step out as you drive the hips (entire upper body) forward with a strong push-off the inside (rear)

The Side Lunge (figures 5-17)

Figure 5.17-a   Figure 5.17-b

leg. This will give you the feel of the push-off and driving the hips at the same time as you step out. Return to the initial position and repeat.

The Reverse Trunk Twist

The reverse trunk twist is one of the best exercises you can do to develop midsection flexibility and strength of the abdominal oblique muscles. They play an important role in keeping the hips and shoulders from rotating excessively in running. When you can do the reverse trunk twist effectively with fairly straight legs, you will have the ability to turn the hips and legs in one direction while your upper body is rotated a full 90 degrees or more in an opposite direction. This ability is extremely important in all forms of cutting. The reverse trunk twist is also a great back stretch and it firms and slims the waist.

Execution

Lie face up on the floor with the arms out to the sides and the palms down. Your arms should be perpendicular to your trunk so that your body forms a letter "T" Raise your legs (thighs) to a 90-degree angle to the floor (see Figure 5.18 a,d). When you are ready, lower your legs to one side while continuing to hold the 90 degree angle in the hip joints.

The Reverse Trunk Twist (figures 5-18)

Figure 5.18-a

Figure 5.18-b

Figure 5.18-c

Figure 5.18-d

Figure 5.18-e

Figure 5.18-f

Touch the floor with the outside of your lower foot (see Figure 5.18 e,f) if you keep your legs relatively straight (more difficult) or with the outer knee (see Figure 5.18 b,c) if you keep the legs tightly bent (easier). Keep your shoulders and arms in full contact with the floor at all times. Inhale and hold your breath as you raise the legs back up to the initial position and without stopping, over to the opposite side until you touch the floor once again. Exhale as you lower the legs and then inhale and hold your breath as you raise the legs. Repeat in an alternating manner.

Russian Twist

This exercise is more advanced than the reverse trunk twist and is used to duplicate the shoulder rotation that takes place in a cutting action while keeping the hips stable. By doing this exercise, not only will you develop greater midsection flexibility, but also greater strength of the abdominal oblique muscles. An added benefit is that it will improve the force of your kicks.

The Russian twist is for players who have adequate strength of the lower back and abdominal muscles. To do this exercise without assistance, you should use a Yessis Back Machine. This is the only machine that has the adjustability needed to fit all body types and sizes.

Execution

Adjust the unit so that when you sit with your pelvis directly on top of the rounded seat, your legs will be straight when your feet are placed between the rollers. Lower your trunk backward to the horizontal position so that your entire body is straight and basically parallel to the floor. Raise your arms so that they are perpendicular to your trunk (see Figure 5.19 a). If a Yessis Back Machine is not available, use a sturdy table and have someone hold your legs down.

Russian Twist (figures 5-19)

Figure 5.19-a

Figure 5.19-b

Figure 5.19-c

When you are ready, rotate the shoulders to one side a full 90 degrees and then back, continuing the movement up and over to the other side until your arms are once again parallel to the floor (see Figures 5.19 b,c). Alternate the right and left shoulder rotation movements until you have completed the desired number of repetitions. Hold a light weight in your hands for greater resistance.

In this exercise, you must hold your body in proper alignment at all times. If you find yourself weakening and your back hyperextending, then immediately stop doing the exercise. In this, as in other rotational exercises, when you rotate with your spine in a flexed or hyperextended position, there are great shearing and compression forces that may injure the spinal discs or vertebrae. Always maintain the natural spinal curvature.

Hip Rotation

The ability to rotate your hips in one direction while facing another direction is a key element in all cutting actions. Players who can easily rotate the hips are said to have swivel hips, the key to faking out your opponent. One of the simplest hip rotation exercises is done with the Active Cords.

Execution

Attach the non-slip Active Cords belt around the hips and secure it firmly. Attach one end of the Active Cords to the ring in front of the right

Hip Rotation (figures 5-20)

Figure 5.20-a   Figure 5.20-b

hip or right on the right hip and stand with the right side in line with the attachment of the other end of the tubing, approximately hip height. When you are ready, shift your weight onto the left leg (slide your hips forward) to create more tension in the tubing. As you do this, turn (rotate) your hips to the left against the resistance of the tubing (see Figure 5.20 a,b). Keep your head and shoulders in place so that the action is isolated to the hips.

The above explanation is for rotating the hips to the left. To develop the muscles for rotating the hips to the right, execute in the opposite manner (i.e., attach the rubber tubing to the left hip and stand with your left side to the stationary attachment.)

Medial Hip (Leg) Rotation

In this exercise you strengthen the medial rotators of the hip joint which are the main muscles involved in rotating the hips to the left when the hips are in motion. This exercise isolates the action to only the left hip joint when it is in support. It can also be done to strengthen the medial rotators in the right hip joint when the right leg is in support and you rotate the hips to the right.

Execution

Assume a seated position, with the legs apart and out straight. Attach the ankle strap around the ball-toe area of the foot and the other end of the Active Cord to a stationary low object. Keep the leg straight and rotate it outwardly as far as possible. This is the beginning position. When you are ready, inhale and hold your breath and lock the leg in place so that it remains straight. Then rotate the entire leg inwardly so that the foot will be pointed inward at the end of the ROM (see Figure 5.21a,b).

Lateral Hip Joint Rotation

This exercise is most important for strengthening the muscles involved in rotating the hips when executing a cutting action. It will make your cuts more effective especially when executing a feinting action.

Execution

This exercise is done in the same manner as above, except that the cord is attached to the inside of the foot and you rotate the leg outwardly rather than inward as above. Be sure to start with the toes pointed in as far as possible and then rotate the leg outwardly as far as possible. Be sure to keep the leg straight at all times. See figure 5.21c,d.

Medial Hip Rotation (figures 5-21)

Figure 5.21-a

Figure 5.21-b

Figure 5.21-c

Figure 5.21-d

Ankle Joint Abduction

This exercise is needed to strengthen the ankle muscles that are used in the cutting action push off, that play a role in stopping forward momentum and which allow for full foot ground contact to prevent slipping. In addition, the muscles, tendons and ligaments involved are the ones typically injured in ankle sprains. Thus, doing this exercise can help prevent injury to the ankle.

Ankle Joint Abduction (figures 5-22)

Figure 5.22-a   Figure 5.22-b

Execution

Assume a seated position with the leg straight and one end of the Active Cord attached to the ankle strap on the inner side of the mid-foot (arch and instep) area. The other end should be attached low to the floor and there should be tension in the tubing in the beginning position.

When you are ready, keep the foot vertical (foot square to the shin), and turn the sole of your foot to the inside as far as possible. In this starting position there should be ample tension on the tubing. When you are ready, turn the sole of the foot outward as far as possible. Do not rotate the shin so that the toes point out as you turn the foot sole outward. When you complete the exercise with one foot, switch the ankle strap to the other foot and repeat (see Figure 5.22 a,b).

Ankle Joint Adduction

This action is the opposite of ankle abduction. It plays a major role only when cutting off the inside leg which, as brought out earlier, is not the best way to cut. Ankle joint adduction also helps to prevent ankle sprains when the ankle collapses to the inside and is used on some kicks.

Execution

Execution is the same as in ankle abduction except that you sit with the Active Cords attached to the outside of the foot. You then turn the sole of the foot inward against the resistance of the tubing. All other directions are the same as in ankle abduction (see Figure 5.23 a,b).

Ankle Joint Adduction (figures 5-23)

Figure 5.23-a   Figure 5.23-b

Resistive Breathing

This exercise is used to strengthen the inspiratory and expiratory muscles which in turn, delay the onset of fatigue, improve cardiovascular endurance and increase Vo2 max. The major muscles involved in inspiration are the diaphragm and intercostals located between the ribs. In expiration the internal and external obliques and the transverse abdominis are involved. To most effectively strengthen these respiratory muscles you must use a resistive device such as The Breather. With this device you can adjust the resistance for inhalation and for exhalation to better match your capabilities.

To exercise the muscles, forcefully inhale against the resistance and then exhale forcefully against resistance at a steady rhythm for up to one minute. Then relax for a minute and repeat (see Figure 5.24 a,b). The breathing can be modified to match different conditions. For example, in sprinting when there is some breath holding you can forcefully inhale, hold the breath, forcefully exhale and so on. Since one of the key actions in breathing is forceful exhalation you should concentrate on greater development of this ability. The faster and more forcefully you can get the air out, the more quickly you can take in air for a more effective exchange of gases in the lungs. Strengthening the respiratory muscles is also very beneficial to players who have asthma.

Resistive Breathing (figures 5-24)

Figure 5.24-a

Figure 5.24-b

6

Specialized Explosive Exercises

The explosive power seen in sprinting and cutting comes mainly from leg and hip joint actions. To increase the ability of these muscles to contract explosively, it is necessary to do speed-strength exercises, i.e., exercises that combine speed with strength. This is the key to increasing explosive power, running speed, and quickness, especially after you have gained strength from doing the specialized strength exercises and have good technique.

Speed-strength or explosive training for running and cutting entails some form of jumping or receiving and repelling a force. In essence, your body receives a force as for example, in a jump landing after which you leap up, i.e., you repel the force. Because they duplicate these actions, many of the explosive exercises used to improve speed and quickness also improve jump height. Before going into the exercises used to develop explosive power it is important to understand that how you jump is critical to the development you receive.

When you do easy jump activities such as simple hopping and skipping, technique is not critical. But as the jumps become more powerful, i.e. the higher and/or the further you go on each jump, how you take off and how you land becomes extremely important. These factors play a key role in the development that you receive and in regard to injury prevention. Following is a brief summary of effective maximal jumping.

The Takeoff

Jumping requires the coordinated action of the legs, trunk and arms. Before jumping upward, you must first go into a partial squat by flexing at the ankle, knee and hip joints. In this slight "crouch," you place the leg and hip extensor muscles that are used in the upward jump on eccentric stretch and they become tensed. The eccentric contraction switches to an isometric contraction when the downward movement is stopped in preparation for the upward movement at which time the muscular contraction switches to concentric. The faster the changes in these muscular contractions take place, the higher you will jump and the more forceful and explosive will be the muscular contraction.

As you approach the bottom position, you should whip the arms down and then up. This circular arm movement places a greater load on the leg muscles so that they contract with even more force in the takeoff. When you then raise the arms and trunk, you raise the center of gravity of the body and the body becomes momentarily lighter. As a result, when the muscles contract with the same force as when you were "heavier", they propel you higher because you are momentarily "lighter". Note that many soccer players, in an effort to avoid arm contact with the ball, do not use the arms to jump upward. Thus you may not have a circular arm movement.

In straightening the legs in the jump, the leg joint actions overlap one another to some extent, but the ankle joint extension should always be the last action to take place. It contributes substantial force to the jump when it is the very last action after the body and legs are completely extended. First should be hip extension followed by knee extension, and then ankle extension. As you leave the ground, the legs should be fully straightened, the trunk should be straight in line with the legs, and the arms can either be overhead, shoulder level or below. The exact height is not important when striving to improve leg explosiveness.

In the initial stance, your feet should be directly under the hips so that when you straighten your legs they push the hips and the upper body straight upward. If you place your feet wider than hip width apart, when your legs extend the forces created will cross your body. As a result, only a portion of the forces generated will be used to raise your body. The remaining force will be wasted since it goes sideways. Keep this in mind when pushing off in running and cutting. Think in terms of pushing the hips forward, not the head and shoulders.

The Landing (Touchdown)

When preparing for touchdown, your feet should be directly under the hips so that the landing forces can be handled efficiently by the muscles in both legs. Landing on only one leg from a relatively high height can be highly dangerous since the forces are twice as great in comparison to landing on both legs. Landing should take place on the ball of the foot, followed immediately by the heel (almost on mid-foot). At this time the ankle, knee, and hip joints undergo flexion. Do not land with the toes pointed so that you land on the ball of the foot close to the toe area. In this position there can be excessive jamming of the foot bones that can create various foot problems. The key to a safe and effective touchdown is to land almost flat-footed so that the ball/heel contact occurs very quickly. This in turn allows for the arch of the foot to do the initial shock absorbing and, more importantly, to withstand most of the landing forces. This is not only the most effective form of landing but also one that will prevent injury.

To prepare for the landing, you should tense the foot and leg muscles slightly while still in the air. In other words, mentally and physically prepare for touchdown before actually making contact. When you do this, as soon as you make initial contact, the muscles and tendons will be engaged immediately and they will be able to keep you from going too low and dissipating the forces generated. In fact, when doing a repeat jump, the less you go down and the faster you leave the ground, the higher you will jump. This is due to the utilization of the energy accumulated from the landing forces for give back in the takeoff. The ability to accumulate energy and to quickly return it is the key to running and cutting faster. This is how jump exercises can improve your running speed and cutting actions.

Many of the explosive exercises described for use in running are also effective in cutting actions. Thus, as you do the exercises for improvement of running speed, you will also be improving your ability to execute faster and better cutting actions (based on your ability to execute effective cutting actions). With poor technique the explosive exercises will have minimal value in improving running speed and cutting quickness.

EXPLOSIVE RUNNING EXERCISES

Explosive Heel Raise

This exercise is basically the same as the heel raise strength exercise except for the speed of execution.

Execution

When positioned with the balls of the feet on the foot platform inhale slightly more than usual and hold your breath as you lower the heels at a moderate rate of speed. As soon as you feel a strong stretch of the Achilles' tendon, quickly reverse directions and rise up as high as possible. Hold the up position for 1-2 seconds and then exhale and repeat. Be sure to make the transition from the down movement to the up movement as fast as possible but smoothly, with no jerking. (See Figure 6.1.) The ROM is slightly less than when doing the exercise slowly or at a moderate rate of speed. See Figure 5.1 in Chapter 5 for more details.

Explosive Heel Raise (figures 6-1)

| Figure 6.1-a | Figure 6.1-b |

Squat Jumps

Squat jumps have two purposes. First they increase your ability to switch the eccentric and isometric contractions to the concentric to ensure a quicker takeoff. Second, they are used to develop greater eccentric strength through a greater range of motion to stop the down action of the body after landing from a jump. This is similar to what occurs when making touchdown in running and especially in cutting actions.

Execution

Assume a standing position with the feet directly under the hips. When you are ready, bend the knees and go into a squat and then explode upward as high as possible. Be sure that the ankles are fully extended and that the legs are straight on takeoff. Prepare for the landing as you are coming down, and then after touchdown, cushion some of the shock and allow the body to go down until there is about a 90-degree angle in the knee joints. Immediately jump up again as high as possible. Be sure that you inhale and hold your breath during the landing and takeoff and exhale quickly when you are airborne. Quickly inhale as you prepare to land and repeat (see Figure 6.2 a-e). To increase the explosive strength component do the exercise holding dumbbells (5-10 pounds) in the hands.

Squat Jumps (figures 6-2)

Figure 6.2-a   Figure 6.2-b   Figure 6.2-c

Figure 6.2-d   Figure 6.2-e

Split Squat Jumps

This exercise improves the power of the takeoff in addition to developing the strength needed for an off-balance or split-leg landing. Ideally you should always land on both feet directly under the hips but many times, depending upon what happens when you are airborne, this becomes impossible. Thus, you should prepare yourself for landing on one foot or with the feet spread apart to prevent the chances of injury. This occurs in running and cutting actions.

Execution

Assume a standing position with the feet under the hips. If you are prepared for greater resistance, hold a 5-10 pound dumbbell in each hand. When you are ready, go into a slight crouch and then leap up as high as possible. Once you are airborne, split the legs with one leg going forward and one going backward. Hold this position so that you land in the stride position. Immediately after landing, jump back up and scissor the legs to land with the opposite leg in front and behind. Repeat in an alternating manner. The key to successful execution is to leap up as high as possible with full ankle joint extension and straightening of the legs (see Figure 6.3 a-h).

Jump Out of a Squat

This exercise is used to help develop reaction time and to improve your takeoff when getting started in running. It can also be used to improve your quickness when taking the first step in a cutting or reaching action.

Execution

Assume a half squat or slight crouch position. The legs should have approximately a 45-degree angle in the knee joints (measured from the back of the thigh to the back of the shin) and the trunk should be inclined forward slightly. Hold the position for 2-5 seconds and then leap up as forcefully as possibly. After landing, go into the same position and hold, ready to repeat (see Figure 6.4 frames a-d). This exercise should be done with weights when you are stronger and more explosive.

When working on reaction time, have someone give you a signal to start. The signal should be auditory or visual and vary in intensity. For example, the command could be very quiet or loud or in between. When using visual signals, have slight movement of the hand indicate a "go" or use full movement of the hand or other body part to signal the start. When working on quickness, in the first step, instead of leaping directly upward, leap in the intended direction of movement.

Split Squat Jumps (figures 6-3)

Figure 6.3-a

Figure 6.3-b

Figure 6.3-c

Figure 6.3-d

Figure 6.3-e

Figure 6.3-f

Figure 6.3-g

Figure 6.3-h

For example, on the hand signal forward, take a quick first step. If the signal is to the rear, take a quick first step to the rear. The same applies to moving left and right. When done in this manner, you must be ready to react to movement in any direction. You must not anticipate where the movement is going to go. In this way, you will be able to develop the reactive ability needed to keep up with an opponent who tries to evade you with quick actions. In addition, it teaches you how to react to various signals such as movement of the hands, arms, legs, or body, depending upon what your assistant uses to signal you.

Jump out of a Squat (figures 6-4)

| Figure 6.4-a | Figure 6.4-b | Figure 6.4-c | Figure 6.4-d |

DOUBLE LEG JUMPS

This exercise is used mainly to develop explosive power in running and cutting. These are three variants.

Double Leg Jumps in Place
Execution

Assume a standing position with the feet directly under the hips. When you are ready, bend the legs slightly and leap up as high as possible with full extension of the legs. Make sure the legs are straight and the toes are pointed. On touchdown, land close to the arch of the foot, i.e., on the ball and then heel of the foot almost simultaneously. Cushion yourself slightly and then jump up fast. Execute the landing and takeoff as quickly as possible. It must be explosive! Prepare yourself mentally and physically for each landing and takeoff (see Figure 6.5 a-f).

Double Leg Jumps for Height and Some Distance
Execution

This exercise is used mainly for explosive leg power directed upward and forward. It is also great in the warm-up prior to sprinting.

Double Leg Jumps in Place (figures 6-5)

Figure 6.5-a

Figure 6.5-b

Figure 6.5-c

Figure 6.5-d

Figure 6.5-e

Figure 6.5-f

Execution is the same as in double leg jumps in place, except in the take-off you incline your body forward slightly so that after you leap up you will come down approximately 12-18 inches in front of the take off spot (see Figures 6.6 a-f).

Double Leg Jumps for Distance (Bounding)

Execution

Execute as in the regular double leg takeoff for height except that you incline the body forward at a 45-degree angle at takeoff. Be sure the legs are fully extended on takeoff staying low to the ground. Upon landing, execute the next takeoff as quickly as possible. If you find yourself sinking too low and the jump taking too long to execute, cut down on the distance (see Figures 6.7 frames a-g). Be sure to jump more for distance, not height.

Double Leg Jumps with Forward Movement (figures 6-6)

Figure 6.6-a Figure 6.6-b Figure 6.6-c

Figure 6.6-d Figure 6.6-e Figure 6.6-f

Double Leg Jumps (figures 6-7)

Figure 6.7-a

Figure 6.7-b

Figure 6.7-c

Figure 6.7-d

Figure 6.7-e

Figure 6.7-f

Figure 6.7-g

SINGLE LEG JUMPS

This exercise is used to improve your ability to land and take off on one leg as occurs in running and cutting. Continual landing on one leg after a jump is not recommended as the forces are twice those of landing on both legs and can be up to 15 or more times your body weight. These are extremely high forces that can easily cause injury if your muscles are not sufficiently strong. Thus, this exercise is also beneficial in helping to prevent injury. The key to successful execution of this exercise is to leap as high as possible in a vertical direction and to execute the landing and takeoff as quickly as possible.

Single Leg Jumps In Place
Execution

Stand on one leg in a well-balanced position. When you are ready, swing your arms down and around and then up. As the arms come up, drive the swing leg knee upward and at the same time fully straighten the support leg and strongly extend the ankle joint to leap up as high as possible. Prepare for the landing mentally and physically early so that as soon as you make ground contact, you can cushion slightly and execute another quick jump upward (see Figure 6.8 a-g).

Single Leg Jumps in Place (figures 6-8)

Figure 6.8-a

Figure 6.8-b

Figure 6.8-c

Figure 6.8-d

Figure 6.8-e

Figure 6.8-f

Figure 6.8-g

Single Leg Jumps with Forward Movement

Execution

Execution is the same as the single leg jumps in place but the forces are directed slightly forward on each jump. You should land approximately 12-18 inches in front of the initial takeoff point (see Figure 6.9 a-f).

Single Leg Jumps with Forward Movement (figures 6-9)

Figure 6.9-a

Figure 6.9-b

Figure 6.9-c

Figure 6.9-d

Figure 6.9-e

Figure 6.9-f

Jump Out of a Squat On One Leg

This exercise is used to develop greater balance and the ability to start a movement off one leg.

Execution

Assume a half-squat position on one leg and hold for 2-4 seconds in preparation for leaping (jumping out). When you are ready, jump to the opposite side of the support leg as powerfully as possible and land on the same leg. For example, if standing on the right leg, leap to your left and land on the right leg (see Figure 6.10 a-g). Balance yourself then leap to the right or forward or backward landing on the same leg. Do on both legs. The direction of the jump can be changed on each jump.

Jump out of a Squat on One Leg (figures 6-10)

Figure 6.10-a

Figure 6.10-b

Figure 6.10-c

Figure 6.10-d

Figure 6.10-e

Figure 6.10-f

Figure 6.10-g

Leaping

Leaping is used to more closely duplicate the push-off and knee drive. It is a very important exercise to use for improvement of stride length and getting the feel of flying through the air.

Execution

To execute, take a few approach steps and then take off on one leg, leaping forward as far as possible. The swing leg should be bent at the knee and driven forward at the same time as the push-off occurs. The body should remain as low as possible in the takeoff and flight phase. Your airborne position should be almost the same as in sprinting; however, the spread between the thighs should be greater.

As you prepare for the landing, swing the shin forward to straighten the leg and then down and back to once again push yourself forward as

Leaping *(figures 6-11)*

Figure 6.11-a   Figure 6.11-b   Figure 6.11-c   Figure 6.11-d

Figure 6.11-e   Figure 6.11-f   Figure 6.11-g   Figure 6.11-h

Figure 6.11-i   Figure 6.11-j   Figure 6.11-k

forcefully as possible on the opposite leg. Be sure your trunk is erect and that the body is well in front of the push-off leg when ground contact is broken so that the forces are directed horizontally (see Figure 6.11 a-k).

Explosive Knee Drive

This exercise is done in basically the same manner as the knee drive exercise for strength. The only difference is the faster initial speed of execution and greater tension on the tubing (or cable).

Explosive Knee Drive (figures 6-12)

Figure 6.12-a

Figure 6.12-b

Execution

When you are ready, inhale and hold your breath as you start the drive of the thigh forward as quickly as possible. Do not drive the knee all the way up to the level position. The key is to have maximum tension when you first begin the forward movement so that the movement stops when the leg is in front of the body (see Figure 6.12 a,b). For more details, see Figure 5.7 in Chapter 5.

Skip Jumps (Power Skips)

This exercise is used to develop greater leg explosiveness and coordination of the takeoff with a portion of the knee drive.

Execution

Begin by taking a few steps and then push-off the ground on one leg and drive the opposite knee upward at the same time. When you leave the ground, the push-off leg should be fully extended and the swing leg thigh should approach level. Upon landing on the takeoff leg, take a short skip and then jump using the opposite legs for the takeoff and knee drive. Distance and speed of forward movement are not important in this exercise as you should concentrate on maximum vertical height and ankle extension (see Figure 6.13 a-l).

Ankle Jumps

Ankle jumps are very important for ensuring that you use the full range of ankle joint extension as needed in running and cutting. Not

Skip Jumps *(figures 6-13)*

Figure 6.13-a

Figure 6.13-b

Figure 6.13-c

Figure 6.13-d

Figure 6.13-e

Figure 6.13-f

Figure 6.13-g

Figure 6.13-h

Figure 6.13-i

using the ankle and relying mainly on knee joint extension is perhaps the biggest fault that I have found with soccer players when analyzing their runs and cuts. This exercise accentuates the ankle action so that you can then incorporate it in a quick sprint or cut. Prior to doing this exercise you should be proficient in the explosive heel raise exercise as described in Figure 6.1.

Execution

Assume a standing position with the feet directly under the hips. Bend the legs slightly and concentrate on jumping solely with ankle joint extension. The height will not be great since it is necessary to eliminate knee joint actions as much as possible. The range of motion in the knee joint should be no more than 15-20 degrees while the ankle joint goes through the full ROM (about 60-80 degrees). The toes should be pointed downward on every jump and the legs should be straight on takeoff (see Figure 6.14 a-e).

Ankle Jumps (figures 6-14)

Figure 6.14-a   Figure 6.14-b   Figure 6.14-c

Figure 6.14-d   Figure 6.14-e

Depth Jump

The depth jump is an advanced exercise that is used to improve explosive power in the legs. It is valuable for improving your running speed and cutting actions.

Execution

Stand on a raised platform that is between 15-30 inches in height. When you are ready, step out with one leg and then drop straight down fairly close to the platform. The key is to drop down in a straight line so that there are no forward forces to contend with. Prepare yourself physically and mentally for the landing while you are still dropping down. As you make contact with the ground, land almost flat-footed, cushion yourself somewhat and then immediately leap up as high as possible, as quickly as possible. Landing and takeoff should take no longer than .15 seconds (see Figure 6.15 a-g).

Be sure to jump straight up after making contact with the ground. Do not execute any other actions after the jump. The key is to concentrate on the landing and takeoff, not on what you may be doing afterwards.

Depth jumps are a form of shock training. As you drop down from a height your body is accelerating so that, at the moment of contact with the ground, the muscles must immediately undergo a very powerful contraction to stop you from sinking very low and to gain the energy needed to leap up as high as possible. Thus there is a "shock" to the body upon landing. The key is to withstand the landing forces and to minimize the cushioning or absorption of the landing forces. In this way, you can utilize the energy in the shock landing. The secret to success is in how quickly you execute the landing and takeoff. If you find yourself going very deep then you are stepping off from too high a height or you do not have sufficient eccentric strength to slow down and stop before leaping upward. In such cases, do additional strength training for eccentric and isometric strength and lower the height from which you step off.

Height of the takeoff platform is very important. Maximum height for takeoff should be 30 inches in height. Do not go any higher. The forces experienced from higher heights create a tendency to sink too low and force you to execute the takeoff slower than what is called for. Depth jumps are very valuable in your arsenal of exercises but they should be used intelligently.

Depth Jumps (figures 6-15)

Figure 6.15-a

Figure 6.15-b

Figure 6.15-c

Figure 6.15-d

Figure 6.15-e

Figure 6.15-f

Figure 6.15-g

Medicine Ball Throw Forwards

This exercise has a dual purpose. It is used to help improve your running and cutting ability and to get full extension of the body.

Execution

Stand holding a medicine ball in two hands below the waist. When you are ready, bend the knees slightly, incline the trunk and go into a slight crouch. Without stopping, raise the trunk, straighten the legs and leap off the ground. As you take off, keep the arms straight and throw the ball up and forward as high and as far forward as possible. When first starting this exercise get the feel of throwing the ball upward and forward with only the arms and then gradually incorporate the legs. Begin with easy throws and gradually build up to full power (see Figures 6.16 a-e).

Medicine Ball Throw Forwards (figures 6-16)

Figure 6.16-a

Figure 6.16-b

Figure 6.16-c

Figure 6.16-d

Figure 6.16-e

EXPLOSIVE CUTTING EXERCISES

In addition to the previously described running and cutting exercises, there are still other exercises and drills that you can do to improve cutting ability. For example, when the push-off takes place in the cutting action, your leg is often in a side facing position in line your hips. In essence, your lower body is in a side facing position. To duplicate the action involved, you should do double and single leg side jumps.

Double-Leg Side Jumps

The double-leg side jump is a great exercise to use to become familiar with side jumps and to develop the power of the muscles involved. When you learn to do this exercise effectively, you will know how to isolate the lower body in the side to side jumping while the head and shoulders remain basically in place. This is the key to all cutting actions; they take place with the lower body, not the upper body.

Execution

Stand with both feet together or hip width apart in an erect, well-balanced position. When you are ready, bend the knees and then leap up and out to one side while keeping the head and shoulders in place. Only the hips and legs should move out to the side. Upon landing, cushion yourself slightly and immediately jump back to the other side where you were and then repeat in a continuous manner. Be sure to cushion your landing but to also withstand the landing forces to immediately jump in the opposite direction. Keep both legs close to one another and limit the action to the lower body, i.e., from the waist down.

The key to effectiveness in this exercise is to jump as far as possible sideways while still executing the change in direction as quickly as possible. If you find yourself sinking too low in the landing or taking too long to jump back, then you are probably leaping too far to the side. Cut down the distance so that you can have both maximum distance together with maximum quickness. Alternate the jumps to the left and right for up to 10 repetitions (see Figures 6.17 a-i).

Single-Leg Side Jumps

The single-leg side jump is the most important explosive exercise you can do to enhance your cutting actions. These jumps duplicate exactly what occurs in explosive cuts using the outside leg.

Double-Leg Side Jumps *(figures 6-17)*

Figure 6.17-a

Figure 6.17-b

Figure 6.17-c

Figure 6.17-d

Figure 6.17-e

Figure 6.17-f

Figure 6.17-g

Figure 6.17-h

Figure 6.17-i

Single-Leg Side Jumps *(figures 6-18)*

Figure 6.18-a

Figure 6.18-b

Figure 6.18-c

Figure 6.18-d

Figure 6.18-e

Figure 6.18-f

Figure 6.18-g

Figure 6.18-h

Execution

Stand with your weight equally balanced between both legs, spaced about hip or shoulder width apart. When ready, shift your hips to put your weight on one leg and bend it slightly. Then forcefully extend the leg and raise the other (inside) leg as you leap out to the opposite side. Land on the now outside (free) leg and as soon as your foot makes ground contact, cushion but mainly withstand the landing forces and then immediately push off in the opposite direction to land on the opposite leg. In essence, you jump from the left leg to the right leg and then right to left leg in an alternating manner (see Figures 6.18 a-h).

Caution: When doing the double or single-leg side jumps, do not use cones or hurdles to jump over. These obstacles force you to jump up, rather than out to the side which is most important in a quick cutting action and one which allows you to cover more ground. All sideward jumps should be done low to the ground, with very little vertical displacement. Also the hurdles can cause injury if you hit them with the feet during the sideward jump.

When doing side jumps, do not use angled boxes or slopes as on some slide boards and jump boxes. When you use a side-angled surface, when you land, you undergo an opposite ankle joint action from what occurs in a true cutting action when the outside foot is planted on the ground. As a result, such jumping may weaken the ankle and cause injury. It is much safer and effective to do strengthening exercises for the ankle and to execute the cutting action on a flat surface such as the soccer field. This allows for the full range of ankle joint action, which is often very great. If you don't lace the shoe to the foot, your chances of losing the shoe in a sharp cut would be very high. Also, when using the side jumps with angled boxes, the ankle does not go through its full range of motion. Thus, you do not prepare yourself for cutting actions on the ground.

Two-Woman Approach and Cut

This exercise can be used not only to work on your offensive cutting ability, but also on your partner's ability to develop her cutting ability for defensive play.

Execution

Stand about five yards away from the center line (or side line) with a partner on the opposite side on the line also about five yards away from the line. When ready, both of you should walk or jog at the same speed

Two-Woman Approach and Cut (figures 6-19)

Figure 6.19-a

Figure 6.19-b

Figure 6.19-c

Figure 6.19-d

Figure 6.19-e

Figure 6.19-f

Figure 6.19-g

Figure 6.19-h

toward the center line where the person who's designated as being on offense makes a sharp cut in either direction.

Your partner who is opposite you and the same distance from the center line must then quickly react to move out in the same direction to keep up with you. For this exercise to be effective, both of you must be close to the line, i.e., close to each other, when the cut takes place (see Figures 6.19 a-h).

Master this exercise first from a walk, then from a jog and then from a slow run. When first executing the cut, be sure that it is a sharp 90-degree cut. Do not travel forward as you make the cut. Once you master this cut, you can increase the speed of approach and execute sharp or 45-60-degree cuts. Do the drill at faster running speeds only after you have mastered each cut and have improved physical abilities.

Four-Way Cuts

When you have mastered the ability to cut backward, sideward and forward, you can do the four-way cutting drill individually or in a group.

Execution

Assume the ready position (athletic stance) and have a coach or some other person stand facing you. The coach then gives a verbal or hand signal indicating the direction in which you must move (run). Begin running until the coach indicates a change in direction so that while you are moving in one direction, you must execute a cut as indicated. There is no set pattern in this drill. You must learn to execute a cut in any and all directions while in movement in any one direction. Each cut should take place after 2-6 running strides.

Execute for up to 30 seconds, but always stop when you start to get mixed up in the cutting directions. If you have difficulty in executing the changes as the coach gives the signals, it may be advantageous for you to do more individual practice on each of these cuts before trying to execute them at random.

General Recommendations for Explosive Jump Training (Plyometrics)

1. When first starting speed-strength training, keep the intensity low. To increase intensity, gradually increase the height of the jumps or use light weights.
2. Begin with double-leg jumps and then move on to single-leg jumps when ready.

3. Gradually increase the volume (repetitions) of jumping in the initial stages of training. As you move into the specialized period of training, increase the intensity (height) of jumping and decrease the volume. (This is analogous to what you do in the progression of changes in weight training.)

4. When you first start jump training, land on surfaces that are neither too hard nor too soft and are somewhat resilient. For example, use gymnastic and wrestling mats, gym floors, a grassy field, etc. Do not do jump training on concrete.

5. Always execute lead-up or preparatory jumps before doing true full intensity explosive jumps.

6. Land on both feet except when doing single leg jumps. When you land on one foot, you have twice the amount of force in comparison to landing on both feet.

7. In the early stages of training, do only 2-3 explosive exercises for one set of no more than 5-6 repetitions.

8. As you develop the ability to do high intensity jump exercises effectively, add more exercises and sets to the workout and increase the number of repetitions in one set to ten. Do not exceed ten repetitions.

9. In general, do no more than 6-10 consecutive explosive jump exercises especially when doing 2-3 sets each.

10. Be sure that you begin jump exercises after an adequate warm-up and after you have completed the active stretches. All jumps should precede lower body and midsection strength training.

7

Active Stretches

Static stretches are well entrenched in soccer and are practiced by most players. For anyone to suggest that the players should not do such stretches is almost sacrilegious. But if you closely examine not only the research done on static stretches in sports but practical experiences, you will see that static stretches do not truly prepare you for soccer playing nor do they help to prevent injury.

In static stretches you hold a particular position for up to 30 or more seconds to stretch the muscles and connective tissue surrounding the joint being worked. For example, it is not uncommon to see players leaning into a wall to stretch the Achilles tendon and calf muscles for fairly long periods of time or bending over to touch the toes to stretch the hamstrings. The key to successful execution of these stretches is to hold the position while relaxing the muscles as much as possible to get a gradual increase in the range of motion (ROM). These static stretches require muscle relaxation which is needed to counteract the muscle and tendon reflexes that hold back increases in ROM. In addition, the muscles should be warmed up before doing such stretches.

Soccer is a very dynamic sport that requires active and often forceful movements of the legs and arms especially in sprinting. The joint actions in running are ballistic in nature, i.e., they are initiated by a strong muscular contraction to accelerate and place the limb in motion after which it continues on its own momentum. The movement is stopped by contraction of the antagonist muscles. Such ballistic movements create great forces that the body must deal with not only for absorption, but most importantly, for accumulating energy for give-back in the return action.

When you do static stretching, the amount of force being exerted is insignificant. More importantly, during the static stretch the muscles are relaxed, whereas in running and cutting the muscles perform dynamically in both concentric and eccentric contractions. In an eccentric contraction, the muscle lengthens and develops tension to guide the movement and to stop it. The concentric muscle shortening contraction is very powerful in creating the movement. The forces experienced in such movements far surpass those that are experienced in static stretching. As a result, you can never prepare yourself adequately to cope with forceful movements if you do only static stretches. This is one reason why it is not uncommon to find injuries occurring. Substantiation can be found in studies that show static stretches done prior to running do not decrease the number of injuries experienced by runners and other athletes.

The ROM seen in running at fast speeds is determined by how strongly the muscles contract to move the limbs through this ROM. Thus, an active ROM is determined by the strength of the muscles involved not by the amount of flexibility possessed. It is the muscular contraction (concentric) that creates the force needed to move the limb through the ROM. Because of this, your stretches should involve the muscles through the same ROM in which they must operate in running and cutting.

In static stretching, the nervous system is literally knocked out so that it cannot activate the muscles and, thus, ensure adequate stretching. This is why static stretches are so effective for permanent elongation of the tissues and an increase in passive flexibility. But it is contradictory to what occurs in running and cutting. In static stretching, because you must voluntarily relax the muscles to eliminate the stretch reflex, the nervous system does not play a major role.

But, in running and cutting, the stretch reflex is involved in all the major actions. Running and cutting are neuro-muscular activities since they require constant firing of the nerves to activate the muscles to continually produce the leg and arm actions. This is a very active process. Thus to truly prepare the muscles and joints for these activities, you should do some active activity to bring about physical preparation of the muscles and joints involved.

Static stretching to permanently elongate the tissues is desirable if you have a limited ROM due to a shortened length of some component of the muscle-ligament complex. If the ROM is not limited, then the static stretching may be ill advised because the increase in ROM by static stretching may compromise the integrity of the joint. In other words, the excessive stretching may stretch the ligaments and other tissues to such a degree that they no longer are elastic. As a result they do not return to their original shape and size. This may be a reason for the increase in the number of injuries that occur to players.

Stretches that are active in nature truly warm-up and prepare the muscles for action. This is the most important goal of stretching in the warm-up. As the term implies, warm-up means to increase the temperature of the muscle prior to participation. By doing active stretches with involvement of the muscles and joints through a full ROM the muscles warm-up and become prepared for the activity.

Understand that stretching and flexibility training are not synonymous. This is why you should differentiate between the different types of stretching and flexibility exercises in order to perform the most appropriate and effective static and dynamic means of increasing functional ROM. Unfortunately the value of stretching that has permeated the literature is related to increasing joint mobility rather than achieving functional ROM in the hip, knee and ankle joints as they are involved in running, cutting and other soccer skills.

All too often static stretching elongates the tissues while disregarding what is taking place in the joints involved. For example, in the standing toe touch to stretch the hamstrings, you bend over from the hips and waist in an attempt to touch the toes. You remain in the bent over position for 30-60 seconds. But, instead of fully stretching the hamstring muscles, you end up with more stretching of the lower back ligaments.

The standing (and seated) toe touch exercises produce a poor stretch of the hamstrings but are excellent stretches of the lower back ligaments that hold the vertebrae in place. As a result of doing such stretches over a long period of time, you may have permanently stretched back ligaments that create a loosely held lumbar spine. At this time it becomes even more prone to injury. To show you the inadequacy of the standing straight leg toe do the following:

Assume a standing position and lock your back in its normal curvature. There should be slight arching in the lumbar spine. Hold the spine in place via contraction of the lower back muscles and then bend over from the hips, not from the waist. The hips must move to the rear as the trunk inclines forward. In my experiences in working with soccer players, I feel confident that most of you will not get beyond a 60-70-degree forward trunk lean.

Look to see where your hands are when your trunk is inclined forward while still holding the normal curvature of the spine. For most of you the hands will be approximately knee high. If you are capable of touching your toes when the back is rounded, it means that the length of your lower legs is the distance over which you stretched the lower back, not the hamstrings. By holding a bent over from the hips position with normal lumbar spinal curvature (slight lumbar arch) for several seconds, you will feel a much stronger stretch of the hamstring muscles. It should also be noted that bending over from the hips is a very safe way of bending over when desiring to pick up or reach something. Avoid the rounded-back position as much as possible since it can be a major culprit in lower back problems.

Flexibility training should assume the same importance as strength and other types of training and should be integrated into the total training regimen. Active stretches for flexibility should be done well before playing or practicing. Immediately before playing or practicing, active stretches to prepare for playing are most important. If you require additional flexibility, then flexibility training should be done at other times as a part of your total training. Also the flexibility training should be coupled with strength training.

We live in an age of specialization and sports are very specialized. Running is not merely the simple act of going out and moving one leg in front of the other in a cyclical fashion. It is a learned skill that can be made more effective and efficient. The same holds true for cutting. Your performance can be improved greatly with proper training not only in relation to how you run and cut but also in relation to the specific exercises that can be done. This includes active stretches that duplicate what occurs in running and cutting to prepare you for playing.

There are many forms of active stretches that range from relatively simple stretches to very complex, explosive type stretches. However, in all cases active stretches involve muscular work during the stretch. This is needed not only to ensure maximum joint safety but to prepare the muscles for a forthcoming action. Active stretches can involve contraction of muscles to perform a movement that stretches the antagonist muscles or they can be done with gravity providing the force to go through the ROM.

The main muscle contraction regime involved in active stretches is the eccentric. In this contraction the muscle develops tension while the overall length of the tissues increases, i.e., they stretch under tension. For example, when you experience touchdown in running and cutting there is slight flexion in the ankle, knee and hip joints to not only absorb some of the landing forces but to withstand these forces. As soon as the foot hits the ground, the muscles and tendons immediately tense, and in many cases prior to touchdown, to handle the forces and to accumulate energy.

When flexion takes place in the ankle, knee and hip joints during ground contact, the muscles and tissues around these joints tense and stretch to control the flexion (down movement). As the muscles and tissues stretch, they develop more and more tension. Once the tension becomes great enough it stops the movement. When you then push-off to leave the ground, the muscles shorten, i.e., they contract in a concentric contraction. Thus the muscles work in unison. The agonist muscles perform an action and the antagonist muscles limit and stop the action and prepare the muscles for the next action to be performed.

Instead of thinking only in terms of the muscles that need stretching, in order to make the stretch specific to what occurs in running, cutting and other soccer skills, you should think in terms of muscle and joint actions. Doing this will give you a better understanding of how active stretches relate to the key actions that occur and how they not only prepare you for action, but can improve your running and cutting.

ACTIVE JOINT AND MUSCLE STRETCHES
Ankle (and Foot Flexion) Extension

Ground contact and push-off are controlled by the muscles and support structures of the foot (mainly the arch), and shin (mainly the Achilles' tendon and gastrocnemius and soleus muscles). The gastrocnemius is especially important as you increase the speed of running. The soleus is active at all speeds but mainly in slow, prolonged running.

On a mid-foot touchdown, when ankle joint flexion takes place, it is important to have not only strength but flexibility of the foot extensor muscles and tendons, and the support structure of the foot arch. In the takeoff, ankle joint extension (plantar flexion) takes place, controlled by the strength of the calf muscles and Achilles tendon and limited by the ROM possible. The best active stretch to improve the ROM in this action is standing ankle flexion and extension.

The Wall Stretch

Stand with the feet flat on the ground two to four feet away from a wall or post and place your hands against the structure approximately shoulder high. Stand far enough away so that you can feel the stretch on the back of the shin. As you lower the heels to contact the ground (or lean into the wall) you should feel a strong eccentric stretch of the Achilles tendon and calf muscles. Hold the position for about 1-2 seconds and then rise up on the balls of the feet as high as possible, and hold the up position for two seconds. Lower the heels at a moderate rate of speed until you feel the stretch, hold and then again rise up on the balls of the feet and hold. The holding on top is important for concentration on full

Wall Stretch (figures 7-1)

Figure 7.1-a   Figure 7.1-b

ankle joint extension which occurs during the push-off. (See Figures 7.1a, b.) This stretch can also be done on a stair step holding the railing for support.

Leg (Knee) Flexion and Extension

A great range of flexion-extension motion in the knee joint is not necessary for effective running. It is needed more for cutting and kicking. In running, the knee joint undergoes flexion on landing but the less the amount of bending, the more effective the running. Thus achieving a 45-degree angle in the knee joint during the stretch is usually more than sufficient for running, while in cutting, a 90-degree angle in the knee is needed. (Measured from the back of the shin to the back of the thigh.)

The Squat Stretch

To do the squat, which stretches the anterior thigh muscles (quadriceps) stand with your feet hip width apart, feet flat on the ground and with the trunk erect. Lock the lower back in its normal curvature (slightly arched lumbar spine) and then go into a squat. As you bend the knees the hips should move to the rear and the trunk should incline forward while the spine remains stable.

Lower the body (think of lowering the hips) while keeping the normal curvature of the spine at all times. Stop when you reach the thigh level-to-the-ground position or when there is less than a 90- degree angle between the back of the thigh and shin. Rise up, and relax and then

Squat Stretch (figures 7-2)

Figure 7.2-a

Figure 7.2-b

repeat. Be sure that the heels stay in contact with the ground which in, turn, provides an Achilles tendon stretch and ensures that the knees stay over the feet as you lower the body to prevent knee injury (see Figure 7.2 a,b). Note that when you rise up, the muscles work against resistance which can increase strength of the quadriceps.

Contraindicated

The common static quadriceps stretch, also known as the butt kick stretch, is potentially dangerous to the knee. In this stretch the thigh is held vertical (perpendicular to the ground) and you pull the lower leg in to bring the heel of the foot close to the buttocks. This is a potentially dangerous position as you are literally pulling the knee joint apart. Since this position is never assumed in the running stride or in cutting, this stretch is not necessary. When the heel comes close to the buttocks in sprinting and cutting, the knee should be forward of the body which gives the quadriceps more slack so that no additional stretching is needed.

HIP FLEXION AND EXTENSION

Hip flexion and extension play key roles in determining running speed and effective cutting actions. They control stride length, effectiveness of the push-off, running speed and cutting ROM. Thus it is important to have ample flexibility in the hip joints. Hip joint flexion and extension flexibility determines how high the thigh can be raised in running before the leg straightens prior to the pull back and when stepping out in

The Lunge (figures 7-3)

Figure 7.3-a   Figure 7.3-b   Figure 7.3-c

cutting. The greater your hip joint flexibility the greater the separation of the thighs in the push-off in cutting and running and the greater is your running speed and quickness. It may also improve your tackling.

Hip Flexion

The hip joint flexor and adductor muscles are involved in hip flexion. They pull the thigh forward in the initial stages of bringing the thigh forward. The adductors initiate hip flexion and then allow the stronger hip flexors to take over when they are in better position. To stretch the hip flexors do the lunge and to isolate the hip joint adductor muscles do the side lunge, also known as the groin stretch which also plays an important role in a side cutting action.

The Lunge (Hip Flexor Stretch)

Assume a standing position with the feet hip-width apart. Take a very long step with one leg and plant the foot with the toes facing forward. Keep the trunk erect and slowly lower the body (eccentric stretch). Keep the rear leg straight but relaxed, with the body weight supported on the front leg. It will not take long before you feel a strong stretch of the hip flexors.

Hold the down position for one to two seconds and then push-off with the forward leg to reassume the initial standing position. Repeat with the opposite leg. Be sure to keep the torso erect and the rear leg straight but relaxed as you do the exercise. If you lean forward or bend the rear leg you will not get an effective stretch of the hip flexor muscles (see Figures 7.3 a-c).

The Side Lunge

Assume a standing position with the feet shoulder width apart, arms alongside the body. Step directly out to the side and plant the foot at a 45-degree angle to the outside. Keep the torso erect and slowly lower your body so that your weight is concentrated on the forward leg, while keeping the rear (push-off) leg straight. In this position you will feel the stretch in the groin almost immediately. Hold the bottom position for one to two seconds and then rise up and repeat with the other leg (see Figures 7.4 a,b). Be sure to keep the trunk erect and to not lean forward.

Hip Extension

In running, the hip extensor muscles must be actively stretched to prepare them for pulling the leg back and down to make contact with the ground. In cutting, they assist in pushing the hips (body) forward in front to back cutting actions and in raising the torso from a crouch position. These muscles also play a role in relation to how far the swing leg thigh can be driven forward during the push-off without adversely rotating the hips. The hip extensors (the gluteus maximus and hamstring muscles) can be actively stretched in two ways: (1) with active participation of the hip flexors and, (2) with no participation of the hip flexors.

Lying Leg Raises

To do this stretch with active involvement of the hip flexors assume a back-lying position with the arms alongside the body and the legs out

The Side Lunge (figures 7-4)

Figure 7.4-a   Figure 7.4-b

straight. When you are ready, hold one leg straight and raise it up as high as possible but not past the vertical position). Then lower the leg to the floor and raise it up again in a continuous action. When the leg is raised via the concentric contraction of the hip flexors, the hip extensors undergo an eccentric stretch. With every leg raise you should be able to go a little further in your ROM. After doing the stretch with one leg, repeat with the other leg. You can also alternate the legs during execution (see Figures 7.5 a-c).

Lying Leg Raises (figures 7-5)

| Figure 7.5-a | Figure 7.5-b | Figure 7.5-c |

The Good Morning

This active stretch does not involve the hip flexors and uses gravity as the moving force. The good morning exercise "isolates" the action to the hamstrings. (The gluteus maximus is also involved if you go through a sufficiently great ROM.) To execute this stretch, assume a standing position with the feet hip width apart. When you are ready, contract the lower back muscles and lock the lumbar spine in its normal slightly arched curvature. Hold the spine in this position and the legs straight and then bend forward from the hips until you feel a strong stretch of the hamstrings. Push the hips back as you bend forward.

For most players, the incline will be approximately 45-60 degrees forward. Be sure to maintain the normal curvature of the spine when you feel the eccentric stretch of the hamstring muscles and tendons. Hold for one to two seconds. Rise up by contracting the hamstrings concentrically and then relax before repeating. Every time you bend over try to go through a slightly greater ROM (see Figure 7.6 a,b).

Good Morning (figures 7-6)

Figure 7.6-a

Figure 7.6-b

Trunk and Shoulder Joint Flexion and Extension/Hyperextension

The ROM in the shoulder joint is very important for ensuring a full ROM in the hip joints. In essence, you need as much flexibility in the shoulder joint as you do in the hip joint. Thus, prior to running, it is important to loosen up the shoulder to ensure that the arm will be able to go through the full ROM in synchronization with the leg actions. For most runners, there is usually ample flexibility in the shoulder joint to allow full ROM in the shoulder joint flexion (the forward arm drive). To fully loosen the connected tissue and muscles in this action, you should do the front raise.

Rather than doing only the front arm raise, it is more effective to combine it with a back arch (spinal hyperextension). Arching the back is effective for stretching the abdominals and to create a fully extended body position which is so important in running. It is also an effective stretch to counteract the ill effects of prolonged sitting and having a rounded spine. Thus, it will help you not only in your soccer play but also in your everyday activities.

Execution

Assume a comfortable standing position with the feet approximately shoulder-width apart and the arms alongside the body. When you are ready, keep the arms straight and raise them directly in front and over

Trunk and Shoulder Joint Flexion (figures 7-7)

| Figure 7.7-a | Figure 7.7-b | Figure 7.7-c |

head as high as possible. Keep reaching backward so that you arch the lower back. At this time, the hips will move forward. Then lower the arms and let them swing freely on the down phase so they go slightly behind the body and then raise them up again with full trunk extension/hyperextension (see Figure 7.7 a,b,c).

Shoulder Joint Flexion/Extension and Elbow Flexion/Extension

Most players seem to have trouble raising the elbows sufficiently high behind the body to a point where the shoulder joint flexion begins in the arm drive. Thus, it is important to do some stretches to see how far you can bring the arm (elbow) backward and upward to ensure a full range of motion for the forward arm drive. In addition, it is important to get the feel of straightening the arm prior to raising the elbow. To prepare for both of these actions, you should do the following combination stretch.

Combination Stretch

After a forward arm drive, straighten the arm and swing it down and back. As the arm moves back, bend the arm and bring the elbow up. Then swing the arm forward, keeping the bent elbow position and then straighten the arm, swing it backwards, bend and raise the elbow and swing the arm forward in a repetitive motion. This action duplicates what occurs in the shoulder joint during the run (see Figure 7.8 a,b,c).

Shoulder Joint Flexion (figures 7-8)

| Figure 7.8-a | Figure 7.8-b | Figure 7.8-c |

Jogging

Jogging is not a specific stretch but is an excellent activity to warm up the muscles in preparation for running and cutting. Jogging, in this case, means starting to run very slowly and gradually building up speed until you are ready to maintain your running tempo. A short jog can precede the stretches if desired. The main jog (run) with a gradual build up in speed should follow the stretches.

By doing the above active stretches you activate the muscles much like what occurs in the running and cutting actions. These stretches will prepare you for action, help prevent injury and most importantly, enhance your playing greatly.

8

Common Running and Cutting Errors

If you have read the previous chapters, you should now have a good understanding of what constitutes effective running and cutting. Most likely you have already tried putting into practice some of the changes in technique and are improving your physical abilities by doing some of the specialized strength exercises.

In regard to technique, many women, even though they know what should be done and believe that they are doing it, are still not capable of carrying out the exact movements. For example, after analyzing the technique of several girls, I took them through some of the changes to be made in each of the actions. One girl thought she was doing all of the movements as directed, but they were far from what was recommended. In her mind, though, she was doing exactly what she was told.

More specifically, the recommendations were to execute the pawback action faster and through a greater ROM. She had a slight amount of pawback, but touchdown still occurred too far out in front of the body and the leg was not brought back with force. As a result, at touchdown, when the foot made contact with the ground, it was very passive and did not lend itself to quick acceleration-type sprints as needed in the game.

To make the change more effective, I had her do the pawback exercise with Active Cords and the standing and walking wheeling (circling) drill. In doing the exercise, she was told to concentrate on the movements so that she would develop a muscular feel for what happens in the pawback action. In other words, not only did she do the exercise for strength, but also for the feel of the movement. To develop the neuromuscular feel for the action, I had her do more repetitions. Once she felt the movement and had sufficient strength to execute it well, it was then incorporated into the total running technique. Only in this way was she able to make the necessary changes to improve her running actions.

In my work with many soccer players over the years, I have found that doing such exercises has been the key to bringing about positive changes in both running and cutting technique. In addition, I have found that most women experience the same or similar deficiencies in their running and cutting which should also apply to many of you. To help you correct there "errors", I have compiled the most common and present them here with their solutions. By doing the recommended exercises and drills, it can make your running and cutting as effective as possible. The exercises are described in detail in Chapters 5 and 6.

ERROR: *The Heel Hit (with the foot angled upward)*

The heel hit, depending upon how it is executed, is not always a major detriment to running. The major fault is when you land on the heel with the foot angled upward. The greater the angle of the foot upward when the heel makes contact, the greater the braking forces and the greater the potential for injury. If, however, you have some pawback and make contact on the heel very close to the arch of the foot, the braking forces are not very great and, thus, in slow running, it is acceptable. However, keep in the mind, the more you can land on the total foot or ball-heel immediately, the more effective your run will be. (See Figure 3.2 frame 6, and Figure 3.8 frames 7 and 8, and Figure 3.9 frame 7 for the heel hit.)

CORRECTIONS:
- Jogging, landing on the balls of the feet first. Emphasize bringing the knee or the thigh in front of the body and then making contact on the ball of the foot. The legs and feet should feel "springy."
- Execute the pawback action while jogging. After swinging the swing leg forward, forcefully bring it back and down to make contact on the ground on the whole foot or ball-heel immediately. The key here is to bring the leg backward prior to touchdown. Do not simply bend the knee or keep the leg bent to land on mid-foot as some runners do. (For example, see Figure 3.3 frames 6-8, Figure 3.4 frames 6-8.) This latter technique still creates braking forces because the foot is in front of the body on touchdown.
- Also helpful is to work on the circling or wheeling drill in which you raise the thigh, swing the lower shin out, and then drive the straightened leg back (see Figure 8.1 frames a-e). Do in a stand-

ERROR: The Heel Hit (figures 8-1)

Figure 8.1-a

Figure 8.1-b

Figure 8.1-c

Figure 8.1-d

Figure 8.1-e

ing position then in a walk and then gradually incorporate this movement into a slow run and eventually into your normal run.

- Do the pawback exercise emphasizing the down and backward movement of the leg (see Figure 5.8 frames a,b for description).

ERROR: *Pushing off with full extension of the leg*

This is seen by a stiff, straight leg during and immediately after the push-off. By fully extending the leg, you are leaping more than maintaining a steady run. It creates longer flight time, which detracts from your speed (see Figure 3.7 frame 5).

CORRECTIONS:

- Emphasize the ankle joint extension while keeping the push-off leg firm but "relaxed" when running.

- Ankle jumps in place (see Figure 6.14 for details).
- Heel raises with a two-second hold at the top of the movement. Execute explosively (see Figure 6.1 for details).

ERROR: *Excessive forward lean of the trunk*

A forward lean is needed only when accelerating. Since you must execute many short dashes, you will probably use the forward lean to a great extent. However, after the first ten yards or so, if you must run further then it is important that you run with an erect trunk. This allows for greater and more effective hip joint action to swing the thighs forward and backward. When in full stride, a slight 1-5 degree of lean is acceptable but no lean is most effective. See Figures 3.2, 3.4, 3.5, and 3.6 for an example of runners who are basically erect and Figures 3.1, 3.3, 3.7, 3.8, and 3.9 for runners who have a slight or noticeable forward lean when in full stride.

CORRECTIONS:
- Maintain an erect trunk position while jogging and running.
- Do the lunge exercise making sure that the rear leg is straight but relaxed as you take a long stride to stretch the hip flexors which are often too tight and pull the trunk forward.
- Execute back raises and the glute-ham-gastroc raise (or hip extension) to strengthen the lower back and hip joint extensor muscles (see Figures 5.10 and 5.9, respectively). They play the major role in maintaining the erect position.
- If back raises are not done, you should do back arches on the floor for creating an arch in the lower back.

ERROR: *The swing-leg knee does not rise sufficiently high during the drive phase*

The main reason this occurs is that the forward knee is not sufficiently forceful and does not move in a horizontal direction. The exact height of the thigh is determined by how powerfully the thigh is driven forward. It is a resultant position determined by the speed of running, not one that you should actively strive to achieve. For example, look at Figures 3.3, 3.4, and 3.7 to see runners who have a forceful push-off but the thigh does not rise to the height that it should in relation to the force of the pushoff. In such cases, there is little concentration in pulling the thigh forward. Most concentration is on the push-off.

CORRECTIONS:

- The forward knee drive exercise with Active Cords and the lunge with resistance of the Active Cords. Be sure that your leg is as far behind your body as it is in the actual running stride and that the movement is executed forcefully. If the push-off leg is not sufficiently behind the body, it indicates lack of flexibility in the hip joint which can be corrected by doing the lunge exercise. See Figure 5.7 for the knee drive and Figure 5.6 for the lunge.

ERROR: *Too much up and down motion*

The more the vertical movement of the body during the run, the less efficient is your run. The vertical movement requires not only more energy but it detracts from forward speed and brings on early fatigue. This is seen most often with heel hitters or when landing with the foot in front of the body.

CORRECTIONS:

- The main reasons for too much up and down motion during the support phase, is usually lack of strength in the quadriceps muscle. To correct this problem, you should do the squat and delay squat (see Figure 5.5).
- The problem may also be due to not executing the pawback action and have a severe heel hit. In this case, the foot lands in front of the body which takes longer for your body to move over the support leg so that when push-off occurs, it drives the body upward instead of forward. The correction in this case, would be pawback exercise (see Figure 5.8).

ERROR: *Short stride length*

This is usually due to a short or weak knee drive, little or no pawback and weak ankle joint extension. Hip joint flexibility may also play a role. This error is seen most often when you attempt to have greater turnover, i.e., take faster steps, by cutting down on the length of each stride. See Figures 3.3, 3.4, 3.7, 3.8, and 3.9 for examples of shortened strides.

CORRECTIONS:

- The lunge exercise with Active Cords (see Figure 5.6 for details).
- The knee drive with Active Cords, beginning with the thigh well behind the body (see Figure 5.7 for details).

- Greater concentration on ankle joint extension and driving the hips forward when running.
- The leaping exercise (see Figure 6.11 for details).

ERROR: *Leg recovery is too high so that you "kick your butt"*

Raising the foot so high that it comes close to touching the buttocks when the thigh is almost vertical is wasted energy and slows down forward leg movement. When sprinting, the heel does come close to the buttocks, but the knee should be well in front of the body. For example, look at Figures 3.1, 3.2, and 3.9. In these figures it is possible to see how the runners are trying to "kick themselves in the buttocks," which indicates that they are not relaxing the leg after the push-off to economize on energy. Instead they actively engage the hamstring muscles to raise the shin.

CORRECTIONS:
- When running, emphasize a strong thigh drive in the push-off and, at the same time, relax the leg muscles, especially the hamstrings (see Figure 5.7 for details). The shin should rise automatically in relation to the push-off force. Instead of continuing upward, the shin moves forward if you concentrate on driving the thigh forward.
- The leaping drill. You must emphasize the push-off together with a strong knee drive during which the lower leg becomes relaxed (see Figure 6.11 for details).

ERROR: *Passive foot strike*

Some players have a good knee drive, swing the shin forward and then leave the leg in front and await contact with the ground. Doing this not only takes valuable time which decreases your running speed, but it invariably leads to a heel hit (or whole foot, if the knee is bent), which slows you down and leads to other problems. See Figures 3.3 frames 6-8, 3.4 frames 6-8 and 13-15, 3.6 frames 6-8, 3.8 frames 7-9, and 3.9 frames 7-9.

CORRECTIONS:
- Concentrate on whipping the extended swing leg back immediately, i.e., execute the pawback action vigorously.

- Do the pawback exercise trying to develop the feel of a one-motion forward swing out followed by the pawback (see Figure 5.8).

- You may also want to do the circling or wheeling exercise, concentrating on making a smooth transition from the shin swing out into the pawback and touchdown. Concentrate on the leg straightening and pulling down phase but do not kick the foot out (see Figure 8.1).

ERROR: *Keeping the elbow at a 90-degree angle when sprinting*

In sprinting, when the leg is in full support, the arm should be straightened to slow its movement and at the same time create more ground reaction forces that can be given back in the push-off (see Figures 3.1 frame 1, 3.2 frame 9, 3.4 frame 9, 3.6 frame 2, and 3.9 frame 4 to see the arm straightening action). Only long distance runners should keep the elbow flexed at a 90-degree angle. Sprinters must use the arms in coordination with the legs.

CORRECTIONS:
- Triceps extension. To strengthen the triceps in a pull down action. See Figure 7.8 a,b, but do with Active Cords. Tubing should be attached high to create the necessary resistance.

- Straight arm pull down with Active Cords. These exercises strengthen the arm and shoulder muscles responsible for straightening and driving the arm downward. (Execute as in Figure 7.8, but keep the arm straight as you pull down from shoulder level to alongside the body.)

ERROR: *Excessive shoulder rotation*

Be sure to distinguish between excessive shoulder rotation and excessive arm swinging across the body. Usually the two go hand-in-hand and the cause is shoulder (and/or hip) rotation. These actions are usually due to excessive hip rotation in order to run in a straight line (see Figures 3.12 and 3.15).

CORRECTIONS:
- To correct this problem, it is important to strengthen the muscles of the midsection. Most important here is the reverse trunk twist, and the Russian twist. In some cases, the back raise with a twist may also be needed (see Figures 5.18 and 5.19, respectively).

ERROR: Inadequate stride frequency

Stride frequency typically depends upon the explosiveness of the muscular contractions especially in the push-off. In general, the shorter the period of ground contact, the greater the stride frequency. This is as common an error as inadequate stride length.

CORRECTIONS:

- Jump and plyometric exercises. Jump and plyometric exercises are most effective for decreasing ground contact time. The key in execution of these jumps and exercises is to minimize ground contact as much as possible, i.e., execute the exercises explosively. Also, do additional strength training exercises for even greater increases in explosiveness (see Figures 6.2-6.10 and 6.13-6.16).

ERROR: Slow first step in accelerating

When in a ready position, especially when the direction of movement is known, it is important that you immediately step out. However, many girls actually take a small step backward then a short step with the opposite leg which they then use to push-off to get into the running stride. For maximum quickness, it is important that your forward leg be immediately driven forward and that you push-off with the rear leg. There will be slight backward movement of the heel, but you should not take a step backward before moving forward (see Figures 8.2 and 8.3 for examples of taking a small step backward and not driving the forward leg to get into the running stride).

CORRECTIONS:

- Practice pushing with the rear leg and stepping forward with the front leg as quickly as possible. Most helpful is to lean into the direction of your acceleration. This is especially important when you can anticipate the direction of movement. Your weight should be moving forward before you actually start the push-off. In this way, your forces are directed more horizontally rather than vertically. Also helpful, is the knee drive exercise and the explosive heel raise (see Figures 5.7 and 6.1, respectively).

CUTTING ERRORS
ERROR: Taking more than one step to stop before cutting

This is a very common error and usually occurs when the player does not know proper technique or does not have sufficient strength to execute the stop on one leg. See Figures 4.3 and 4.4 to see how the player

ERROR: Slow First Step in Accelerating (figures 8-2)

Figure 8.2-a

Figure 8.2-b

Figure 8.2-c

Figure 8.2-d

Figure 8.2-e

Figure 8.2-f

stops first on the right inside leg and then the left outside leg before making the actual change in direction.

CORRECTIONS:
- To learn effective cutting technique, see the descriptions of cutting actions in Chapter 4.
- When there is insufficient strength of the outside stopping and cutting leg, you should do the squat and delay squat (Figure 5.5).

ERROR: *Not raising the inside leg when planting the outside foot*

This error typically occurs when the player does not have sufficient strength to stop on one leg. In essence, she must use both legs to create the stopping forces. When you stop on both legs, it takes longer to make the change and to step out to cover more ground as you pushoff on the

ERROR: Slow First Step in Accelerating (figures 8-3)

Figure 8.3-a

Figure 8.3-b

Figure 8.3-c

Figure 8.3-d

Figure 8.3-e

Figure 8.3-f

first step. See figure 4.4 and 4.7 to see both feet in contact with the ground during the cut.

CORRECTION:
- The most important correction that can be made is learning technique to stop on one leg so the inside leg is free to move out quickly.
- Also important is to strengthen the quadriceps muscle to create a stronger braking action on one leg so that the inside leg can be lifted freely (see Figure 5.5 for details on the squat).

ERROR: Not stepping out with the inside leg when taking the first step

This action may be due to not knowing the proper technique especially if you have been taught to crossover when starting to run, which takes more time. It is important that you learn to step out with the inside leg in the very first step as you pushoff so that you cover more ground and get into the running stride faster. For example, see Figure 4.3, frames 6-7. Even though her inside leg is free as she begins to push-off, she puts the free foot down on the ground and then crosses over to begin running with the outside leg. A similar situation can be seen in Figure 4.4 where the inside leg remains stationary as she crosses over and then goes into the running stride.

CORRECTIONS:
- Strengthening the hip joint abductor muscles. These muscles are used to initiate the forward movement of the leg followed by hip flexion especially if you turn the hips early. For details on the hip abduction and hip flexion exercises, see Figures 5.14 and 5.7, respectively.

ERROR: *Leaning over the outside leg*
Almost all the girls pictured do not lean over the outside leg. Coming close to doing this is the girl in Figure 4.5, frame 4. However, this is a common error, especially with young girls who haven't mastered the ability to stick the leg out in front while maintaining the upper body in place. Thus, most important for correction of this problem, is to learn proper technique. Sometimes the leaning over the outside leg may be caused by inadequate strength of the mid-section muscles to hold the trunk rigid and in place.

CORRECTIONS:
- Read Chapter 4 for description of the various cutting actions in order to learn how to execute the cut without leaning over the outside leg.
- To strengthen the midsection muscles, it is necessary to do exercises such as the back raise and the reverse trunk twist. These exercises are explained in detail in Figures 5.10 and 5.18.

ERROR: *Not maintaining an erect trunk during the cutting action*
This is seen most visibly in Figure 4.5. It typically occurs as a result of going into a deep body crouch to create sufficient force on the stopping leg to stop forward momentum. In some cases it is due to lack of sufficient mid-section and hip joint strength to maintain an erect trunk.

CORRECTIONS:
- Doing exercises such as the back raise and reverse back raise are most important for maintaining the erect trunk position.
- Doing the pawback exercise or the glute-ham-gastroc raise, is important for strengthening the hip extensors used to maintain an erect trunk. For descriptions of these exercises, see Figures 5.8, 5.9, 5.10, and 5.11.

ERROR: *Not looking forward during the cut (maintaining the same field of vision during the cut)*

This error is very common especially among young players. They typically do not have the physical ability to execute lower body actions while maintaining the same upper body posture. This is visible in Figure 4.8, frames 4-6, Figure 4.9, frames 3-5, and Figure 4.10, frames 4-6. Often combined with not looking forward during the cut is turning the whole body during the cut together with the head. This is visible in Figures 4.4, 4.8, 4.9, and 4.10.

CORRECTIONS:
- Most important is to develop sufficient strength of the mid-section muscles together with midsection flexibility. The best exercise to do this, is the reverse trunk twist (see Figure 5.18). Also valuable, especially in the advanced stages, is doing the Russian Twist (see Figure 5.19).
- Also important is to do exercises specific to hip rotation while keeping the shoulders in place. Such exercises help teach you the feel of the movement of turning the hips while maintaining the head and shoulders in one direction (see Figure 5.20 for details).

ERROR: *Cutting off the inside leg*

This error is not seen in any of the figures in this book. However, it is a common error and usually occurs when running forward and then cutting to one or the other side.

CORRECTIONS:
- To correct this error, it is important that you learn proper technique by learning to cut off the outside leg. In some cases, you have to learn how to adjust your steps so that the cut can be made on the outside leg especially when you know where you will be executing the change in direction.

- It is also important to break the habit of crossing over with the legs when making a change in direction. This typically occurs on a cut off the inside leg. But, when you crossover, the legs put you in a vulnerable position, but it takes longer to execute the cut. Thus, the key is in learning proper technique.

Nutrition for Optimal Playing

9

If you want to be a great player, you must give your body the right fuels to do it. Your diet must satisfy your mouth as well as your muscles and there is a way of eating that will enhance your playing and health. The only "diet" you should be on is the one you can stay on and enjoy for life.

EATING TO BE BETTER

An exercise or soccer training program without the right diet is like trying to run your car without sufficient fuel or oil. Sooner or later the car is going to break down or function poorly, as will your body without the right nutrients. Think of food not as an enemy but rather as an ally and a very important one. Why? Because of a simple phenomenon known as supercompensation. It occurs in response to the training effect, i.e., the results you achieve from your training.

For example, if you play or workout more than you are used to, your body will experience a greater work load than it is accustomed to. As a result, you deplete the body's energy supplies in order to get the work accomplished. After the work is done, recovery begins to take place and some of the energy stores are replaced quickly so that you have enough energy to continue doing various tasks during the day.

The main recovery phase, however, takes place when you are sleeping. It is at this time that the body goes to work not only to repair any damage that was done to the muscles and tissues, but also to restructure the muscles and support structures in response to the playing or training exercises completed. There is replenishment of the glycogen stores which brings your energy levels back up, and many other body functions take place to return your body to a stable state.

161

However, the body does not just compensate for what you have done or merely replace the energy supply that your body originally had. Because the body does not like to be stressed, it deposits additional energy stores so that the next time you do this amount of work the body will have an ample reserve which, in turn, allows you to do even more. This is known as supercompensation, but if you do not do sufficient work, your body will never get to the point of bringing about supercompensation, and you will merely be recovering or replacing what was used up.

You probably experienced supercompensation when you first began to play seriously. After you finished playing one or more competitive games, you were probably quite tired, but as you kept up the playing, in the following days and weeks, you eventually were able to play much longer without undue fatigue. Thus, in the very early stages of playing, your body overcompensated. But once you were accustomed to the game play, your body merely replaced the energy supply that was used up and you once again returned to your normal state.

If you want to improve your capabilities and get a training effect, you have to exert yourself physically more than usual. You need the supercompensation for additional gains in power, speed, strength, flexibility, endurance, and other physical qualities. Supercompensation is your ticket for making progress not only in your playing but in your physical development. But, for supercompensation to occur, your body must have the needed nutrients to make the positive changes possible!

For your soccer and exercise program to be most successful, you must have the nutrients to make the body changes you need, especially during the period of supercompensation. To exercise and play without giving your body these required fuels is just adding one stress to another almost as blatantly as if you were trying to run your car without gas. Eating well is not difficult and does not require extensive record keeping. The key is to not count calories but to choose a wide variety of the right kinds of foods, in the right amounts and eating them at the right time of day.

According to researchers, teenage girls have the worst diets of any group in the United States. But the teenage years are the formative years for many female soccer players. Because of this, it is extremely important that you are not one of the people in this group. If you are, it can severely retard your physical and mental growth and your development as a player. To be able to develop your full potential and to play on the highest levels, you must have a diet commensurate with your playing potential.

FATS

Fat is calorically denser than protein or carbohydrates. A single gram contains nine calories, while a gram of protein or carbohydrate contains only about four. This is why the breakdown of fats provides double the energy of carbohydrates or protein. Diets high in saturated fat and trans-fats however, are a risk factor for obesity, heart disease, high blood pressure, stroke, diabetes, and even some forms of cancer.

A high fat diet of mostly saturated fats typically leaves you feeling sluggish, so that you will not be able to play or exercise at your best. Also dietary fat has a pronounced tendency to become body fat, once consumed. That is especially true of saturated fat, the kind found in fatty meats, full-fat dairy products, palm and coconut oil, and, trans-fats (hydrogenated oils) as found in margarine and many other products, especially processed foods. Studies show that diets high in saturated fat tend to produce body fat in the area of the abdomen and hips more so than anywhere else.

For girls going through puberty, Mother Nature automatically deposits more fat in the area of the abdomen and thighs. If you are not especially careful at this time, in relation to the foods and amounts of foods that you eat, then you may end up with excessive fat in the abdomen and hip area. Once deposited, it becomes exceptionally difficult to eliminate in these areas.

Fat must never be eliminated or severely cut back from the diet if you want to play a full game at your best. This is especially true of the mono and poly-unsaturated fats. The body needs fat for many functions, which include assimilating fat-soluble vitamins and manufacturing cell walls and certain essential enzymes and hormones. It is essential for recovery after severe workouts and for muscle hypertrophy. Fat also helps make food both more satisfying and more filling and it supplies the best energy for continuous playing.

Limit your intake of dietary fat to about 25-30% of your daily caloric intake. Start simply by cutting down on the most obvious foods that contain saturated fats, such as fried foods, rich sauces, hamburgers, hot dogs, full-fat salad dressings, mayonnaise and rich desserts. Use good oils, such as olive, canola, peanut, safflower, flaxseed, or walnut, and be very selective in your use of other fats. These oils play many valuable roles in the body.

An excellent way to get good fats is to eat raw nuts as a snack. Use butter instead of margarine. Even though the virtues of margarine have been extolled for many years, we now know that it results in many more negative effects than does butter. Butter is a natural product that the body can assimilate, while margarine, a trans-fatty acid, acts the same as a saturated fat and remains in your body for extended periods of time. Eat plenty of fish and fish oils, especially if you have a tendency to overdo the saturated fats. The fish oils will help move the saturated fats out of the body.

PROTEINS

Proteins are very important as they provide the basic building blocks for cellular muscular repair and development and provide energy. While carbohydrates and fats supply most of the energy for muscular exertion, protein enables your muscles to respond to this exertion by getting firmer and stronger (and also supply you – especially the brain — with energy!). This is why your need for protein increases the more you put your muscles to work. Exercise causes the muscles to undergo a type of intricate cellular breakdown that only protein can repair and build upon.

Playing soccer and being on a regular exercise program means you should be getting approximately one half to one gram of protein daily for every pound you weigh (approximately 30% of your daily caloric intake). The exact amount will depend upon your age, intensity and duration of the workouts, and your level of development. Some of the best sources of protein are lean meats, poultry, fish, low-fat dairy products, whole-grain cereals and breads, beans and nuts.

Because soccer is mainly a speed-strength type of sport, it requires greater amounts of protein than other sports as for example, endurance sports. Many coaches believe that soccer is an endurance event, but because of the many quick dashes and many stops and starts, it involves more speed-strength rather than pure endurance as for example in a cross-country or long-distance run. Because of this, in some cases, you should increase the amount of protein to over one gram per pound of body weight. The increase in protein dictates a decrease in carbohydrates. In this way, the extra protein allows for the creation of optimal conditions for maintaining and increasing your work capacity.

When you undergo intense loads, as occur during competitive play and in some practices, there is constant wear and tear on the muscles, tendons, and cartilage tissues. The amount of wear and damage to the muscles, tendons, and cartilage is greater in speed-strength type sports than in most other events. Because there are microtrauma and micro tears and sometimes even more serious damage to the tissues, it requires greater protein for repair and rebuilding of these tissues. Only in this way, will the muscles, tendons, and ligaments become more functional and complete.

It is also important to understand that increasing your ability to play longer and harder and more frequently and to play on a higher level, depends not only on your ability to recover, which is tied in with resynthesis of destroyed tissues but also on an increase in muscle mass. The increased amount of muscle allows you to do more work. This does not mean that there must be a massive increase of muscle as in bodybuilding, but enough muscle to allow you to execute more powerful kicks, faster running and quicker cutting actions.

Your ability to recover is only possible with a definite combination of not only training loads, but nutritional foods which should contain increased quantities of protein. In addition to the protein, in order to get the optimal synthesis going which provides tissue restoration and muscle hypertrophy you must have a sufficient amount of vitamins and lipids (fats). If you have a deficiency of vitamins, especially if you eat only small amounts of fresh fruits and vegetables, it can seriously interfere with the protein synthesis. In this case, it is strongly recommended that you supplement your diet with a natural vitamin supplement.

In regard to the lipids (fats), they play an important role in stimulating division of the cells and building cell membranes. Thus, they are necessary both for recovery as well as for muscle growth. If you are lacking the lipids, not only is your appetite decreased, but it makes the functional properties of the cells and tissues worse. As pointed out above, they should comprise not more than about 30% of the total calories in your food intake.

CARBOHYDRATES

Carbohydrates are great for fast energy and in some ways the most healthful type of food you can eat. This includes foods such as pasta, cereals, breads, potatoes, rice, beans, fruits and vegetables. Carbohydrates should be eaten in their natural, "complex" forms. Potato chips and candy bars don't count!

The more energy you have, the more inclined, as well as the more capable you are going to be, to have high quality playing time and workouts. Some carbohydrates are unique; they "rev-up" your body's metabolic rate, even when you're just resting, and once you begin to exercise, carbohydrates really begin to kick into gear. But they are of relatively short duration. If you play and workout for an hour or more, then fats (and some of the amino acids), become most important. The higher the intensity and duration of the playing or workout the sooner you will need to rely on fats.

However, when you do find that you will be playing for long amounts of time, as for example in tournaments in which you may end up playing more than one game a day, then the amount of carbohydrates as well as the other nutrients should be increased. The key here is not so much to use more carbohydrate during play but to have enough carbohydrates available for quick bursts of speed when needed. Keep in mind, that when you execute quick bursts of speed and quick changes in direction, it relies on the anaerobic (without oxygen) processes. The fuel for this comes from your carbohydrates or sugars, but they are used up quickly and thus, you must conserve them as much as possible so that you will have an ample amount not only to last you the full game but also for the number of games that you will be playing.

However, there are exceptions to this information. It seems that rather than being used up immediately for energy, carbohydrates in many women are not immediately burned. In fact, they seem to have the opposite effect, they make the women tired and sluggish. Some doctors strongly believe that it is the carbohydrates that tend to put on more weight with women, rather than being used for energy. Thus, it is important that you closely examine the effects of eating high carbohydrate diets or even a high carbohydrate meal. For example, I know some girls who, after eating a plate of pasta, are ready to go to sleep as opposed to having energy to go out and play.

FIBER

Fiber is the key to keeping your digestive system in shape. But fiber can also affect the shape of your body as well, mainly because fiber plays a role in excretion of dietary fat. Get enough fiber in your diet and you help "sweep" dietary fat through your intestines before it has a chance to be fully absorbed. This spares not only your waistline, but also your arteries and heart. The best sources of fiber are foods rich in carbohydrates (grains, potatoes, beans). Try to get approximately 30 grams of fiber a day, which is more than what most people routinely consume.

EATING HINTS

You don't have to look far to find the kinds of foods that will enable you to function at your best. For example: bread, cereal, rice, pasta, nuts, fruit and vegetables are among the most nutritious foods you can find. Grains are nutrient storehouses. Grains such as wheat, oats, brown rice, millet, rye and barley are rich in vitamins and minerals, and provide great amounts of energy. No wonder that grains, along with beans and legumes, serve as a staple for so many cultures.

To fulfill your quota of valuable complex carbohydrates which take longer to breakdown than the sugars, think beyond the popular white rice and white flour baked goods that have most nutrients removed.

Choose from whole grain products and go for variety. Cornbread, muffins and pancakes made with whole grains and little fat are fine. But avoid fat-enhanced baking goods such as biscuits and high fat quick breads. Read the labels on pastries, taco shells, and pancake mixes for fat content. And stay away from corn chips (except blue corn chips), donuts, potato chips, high fat crackers, cookies, cakes and sweet rolls. Many of these products contain sugar, a simple carbohydrate that is burned very quickly by the body to give you a "high", but which does not last very long.

Vegetables should be a mainstay of your diet. When you make a salad, think beyond iceberg lettuce, which is practically void of any nutritional value. Use two or three different kinds of greens, such as spinach, red lettuce, chicory, escarole or romaine. Add items such as tomatoes, cucumbers, celery, green, yellow or red peppers, red or green onions, broccoli, cauliflower, carrots, or any raw vegetable you enjoy. To further liven up salads, work in some foods from the grains and legumes groups and toss some peas or beans on your greens. Such salads can even be eaten without any dressing which is usually loaded with bad fats. A little olive or canola oil, lemon juice with salt and pepper usually works wonders for additional taste.

In this way, you can consume hundreds of satisfying calories, while taking in minimum amounts of fat. Also keep a couple of sealed plastic bags of raw cut-up veggies handy in your crisper. Broccoli, carrots, zucchini, cauliflower, asparagus, green or red peppers, pea pods, fresh green beans, chickpeas, mushrooms, turnips and tomatoes are great for snacks. The vegetables are very important for getting your vitamins and minerals and for keeping your body systems functioning well.

Fresh fruit can quench your thirst and fill you up. Whole fruit is also a reliable source of fiber and various vitamins and minerals. Go for the whole fruit, preferably locally grown and naturally ripened, since it is more satisfying and nutritious. Fruit in season is more likely to be fresh. Carefully check out of season fruit to be sure it has not gone bad even if it looks good. Because of improvements in preserving fruits (as for example, apples) it is not uncommon to find some in the market that are over a year old! Because of this, you should not get locked in to only a few fruits. Learn to enjoy many different kinds!

Yogurt and cheese are also important in your diet along with meat, poultry, fish, beans, eggs, and nuts. Protein is very important and you should eat mostly lean meats to get your full complement of amino acids with less saturated fat. To fulfill your daily quota of this food group, concentrate on foods rich in high quality protein, such as lean meats, poultry, beans and fish. Fresh raw nuts and seeds are an excellent source of protein, fiber, vitamins and minerals.

In regard to eggs, they are not the culprit in increasing your cholesterol levels. The real culprit is the feed that chickens are fed! The feed is devoid of products such as lecithin, the key to breaking up cholesterol and moving it through the body. In other words, the adulterated chicken food that is lacking in nutrients makes the eggs sources of cholesterol! Natural or fertile eggs from cage-free chickens or chickens fed a vegetable diet will not give you higher levels of cholesterol and are an excellent food.

FAT-FREE FOODS

The number of fat-free foods has increased astronomically over the past few years, as have low-fat substitutes. However, studies show that people now eat more fat than they did before, and are still gaining weight because they are eating more. Thus, the culprit is not simply eating food with fat. It may be eating adulterated foods! Best is to eat food with the fat in its natural state and to not overeat. Avoid processed foods as best as possible. This is not easy as it is rare to find pure unadulterated food in the markets.

Another drawback to eating low-fat and no-fat foods is that the reconstituted versions of the real thing lack fat soluble nutrients and possibly other undiscovered nutrients. Scientists are still discovering new vitamins and minerals that up until now were not thought to be important to human health! To be sure you are getting an adequate supply of everything you need, your diet should include foods that are as close as possible to their natural state. Also, you should learn to substitute good oils for bad fats. For example, put olive oil on your bread instead of butter.

Don't rely on artificial sweeteners. Studies have found that over the course of a year, people who use artificial sweeteners are more likely to gain weight than non-users. The artificial sweeteners may increase feelings of hunger since the brain interprets all sweeteners equally and triggers changes in blood sugar that mimic a reaction to sugar.

KEEP IT SIMPLE

When it comes to preparing food, less is better. Don't overcook vegetables or obliterate otherwise healthy foods with high fat cooking techniques, such as deep-frying, or sautéing in gobs of lard or butter. It has been my experience that foods eaten as close as possible to their natural state provide maximum nutrition and taste with minimum fuss. So do yourself a favor: leave the time-consuming and calorie-adding gourmet cooking techniques to French chefs. Try to appreciate foods for what they are, as opposed to what they become once adulterated by some high-fat garnish or sauce, and you will be that much ahead of the game.

NO MEAL SKIPPING

If you are a serious soccer player, you should eat at least 3-5 times a day. That's right, no meal skipping and especially no fasting allowed. Your body is a finely-turned machine that needs fuel (nutrition) on a regular basis. The next time you are feeling "too busy" to eat, and don't have time for a conventional meal, there is nothing wrong with a healthful snack, such as a piece of fruit, a small sandwich, some nuts or a container of yogurt. Many athletes find that eating 5-6 mini-meals a day gives them more energy during the day.

The use of whole food bars such as the Standardbar that contain a balance of various nutrients, vitamins and minerals are also beneficial, especially when there is insufficient time for a full meal to digest before a heavy practice or competition. However, beware of the food (energy) bars made from synthetic chemicals. They do not have the wholesome food benefits as in whole food bars such as Standardbar and may even have some negative effects.

DRINK LOTS OF WATER

As you probably know, water is extremely important for soccer players. It not only keeps you hydrated enough to play and exercise with maximum efficiency, but it also helps your body cool itself, and get rid of its natural waste products. When you exercise you lose water, not just through sweat but also through your breathing, and the losses can be substantial.

This doesn't mean that sweating is a negative, it is natural and desirable. Perspiration cools the body, gets rid of waste products, and cleanses the pores. But it does deplete the body of water that must be replaced, so play it safe. Drink at least 8-10 eight-ounce glasses of water a day, which does not include soda, beer, coffee or tea. On practice or game days, increase the amount accordingly. (One rule of thumb suggests a liter a day for every 50 pounds you weigh.) And don't wait till you're thirsty to drink. Your body can be short of water without your thirst letting you know about it.

There are also some good bottled waters on the market that can assist you greatly in recovery after a work-out. One such water is OxyWater. It has oxygen added so that it contains between 5 to 7 times that of normal bottled waters. There are no other additives or chemicals, making it an ideal supplement for recovery. Some players even feel that it makes the playing easier because of the resultant greater oxygen saturation in the blood. They also experience faster recovery in between halves and after games.

Recent double-blind studies have shown that not only does OxyWater have a positive physiologic effect but also a noticeable performance effect. Athletes were capable of performing better after drinking some of the OxyWater. Thus, by using drinks such as OxyWater, not only can you help rehydrate the body but also help your recovery and improve your performance at the same time.

EAT FOOD NOT PILLS

I can not overemphasize the importance of eating fresh and natural foods whenever possible. Don't let yourself be duped by the fantastic advertising claims often made for certain high price foods or supplements especially if processed or synthetic. If you eat wisely and eat a variety of foods from the different categories you shouldn't need many additional supplements. Supplementation, as the term implies, is to supplement your diet.

If you find your diet lacking, or your food sources are grown in land that is depleted in nutrients, or if there are environmental conditions that lower the value of foods, then supplementation becomes very important. As for health foods, there are none better than what you can make for yourself from fresh natural organic foods.

When you take supplements, be sure that they are full natural complexes of the various vitamins and minerals. In nature, these vitamins and minerals are combined in varying degrees and should be eaten in their natural forms so that the body can better assimilate them and get their many benefits. Beware of synthetic products and especially synthetic vitamins as they may actually create vitamin deficits in the body and not give you what your body truly needs.

For example, the synthetic version of vitamin C consists of ascorbic acid. But ascorbic acid is only one component of the total Vitamin C complex. In addition to ascorbic acid, the natural Vitamin C complex contains other vitamins and minerals in order to be complete. When you take only ascorbic acid into the body, it will rob the body of other nutrients in order to become complete, and if continued over a long period of time, can deplete you of other vitamins and minerals.

ENJOY YOUR FOOD

With a little imagination and not a lot of work, you can make your healthy diet extremely enjoyable. If your diet isn't giving you pleasure, it is lacking in some aspects, regardless of how nutritionally complete it may be. Important too is allowing yourself some of your favorite foods, because many foods that you "crave" are trying to tell you something about your body's chemistry. A craving for something sweet, for example, could be a sign that your blood sugar has fallen too low. (Don't make this a habit though.) Or a strong urge for something salty could mean that the sweat that you are losing in your workouts has caused your body's sodium levels to dip. Use natural sea salt to make up for any loss.

Learn to respect your body's messages if you are serious about soccer and your health, because they are usually telling you something you should know. If you are exercising regularly, the food will have a purpose. In fact, the more you compete and exercise, the more you will automatically find yourself migrating to better and healthier foods, mainly because you will see the difference in your playing abilities and how you feel.

CARBOHYDRATES OR FATS FOR ENERGY?

As you start your soccer playing or workouts your energy levels are usually high. Initially you utilize a fair amount of the sugars (carbohydrates) that are present in your body from the stores of glycogen. Once you have depleted the sugars your body goes to burning fats. As a result you usually see a difference between the beginning and middle or end of play in regard to not only your playing but how you feel.

If you constantly take in carbohydrate-type drinks and other products to keep replenishing the carbohydrate stores, your body will not be trained to utilize the fats in the body. Fats are not automatically burned most effectively. You must train to have the body adapt to the burning of the fats for high energy. One of the most effective regimes to do this is to play or workout close to your anaerobic threshold and to sustain it as long as possible. In a competitive game you play in this high anaerobic range intermittently. But, if you train close to this threshold, you can get the greatest breakdown of fats which supplies much more energy than carbohydrates per unit of use.

However, if you limit the amount of fat that you take in and keep replenishing the carbohydrates stores by constantly taking in more carbohydrate foods and carbohydrate-type drinks during the workout or during play, your body will limit the burning of fats and, as a result, not be trained to maximally utilize the fats in the body.

Studies have shown that elite men soccer players have their heart rate (HR) around 160-200 beats per minute (bpm) for the entire game. Because of this, it is impossible to replenish the amount of carbohydrates necessary to continuously play in this high zone. The more you use up your carbohydrate reserve, the less you will have for finishing the game or having enough energy to finish the game playing well or at a fast pace. Keep in mind that many times when you start feeling very tired, it is not necessarily because of your cardiovascular or respiratory system fatigue, it may be due to your lack of fuel to keep going. In this case, it is most likely the fact that you have used up your carbohydrate reserve and are now unable to execute quick sprints and cuts that rely on these reserves. The key to playing on a high level is to get your body to the point where you can burn fat more efficiently as the intensity of the work increases.

When you first start playing or practicing you rely on carbohydrates to produce the energy needed. Once your cardiovascular and respiratory systems speed up to balance the work load, you go into a steady state and you begin to burn some fat rather than relying only on carbohydrates. When first starting, you develop what is known as oxygen debt, which you must pay back later in recovery by taking in sufficient oxygen to create more energy (glycogen) to replace the carbohydrates that have been used. This typically occurs during halftime or after a game when you are not active and your body has a chance to recover.

As the intensity increases, you should begin burning more fats until you hit the anaerobic zone which is a HR of about 160 bpm for a typical high-level player. Thus, in your training, it is important to work with your HR close to this level most of time so that you become proficient at burning fats. Note that, as the intensity increases even more into the HR range of 160-180, not only do you burn some fats but you begin to rely more on carbohydrates. This is why, when the intensity increases, you will not be able to last more than a few minutes in the upper range. Because the playing is intermittent, your heart has a chance to drop slightly below or down to approximately 140-160 bpm, so that you can once again rely on the fats for energy and can conserve and build up the carbohydrate reserve.

When the intensity increases to the highest levels, as occurs when you execute a quick dash for ten to fifteen yards, or execute quick cuts and dashes in combination with one another, the HR will be up to 180-200 bpm at which time you must rely solely on carbohydrates to produce the energy needed. When you slow down or stop, carbohydrate use will again diminish if you can burn fats for the energy needed. The more you can spare the use of carbohydrates and save them for all-out high-intensity dashes and cuts, the longer you will be able to play at your best for the entire game without undue fatigue. This is why it is important that you do not over emphasize the use of carbohydrate drinks in practice. They will give you the energy to play at a high level, but you will not be able to duplicate this in a game situation and thus, you will find yourself at a major energy loss.

The fact that the body relies greatly on fats to fuel your overall playing over the course of play, is so obvious that it has been greatly overlooked. In the fitness literature, it is well recognized that if you wish to lose fat you must workout longer and at a faster pace. As a result, your body utilizes more fat for energy and you lose the fat stores. Because of this, I am always amazed at the diets often recommended for soccer players that contain mostly carbohydrates which put off the burning of fats.

For example, recent studies have substantiated that fat is the predominant energy source during prolonged exercise as occurs in soccer play. Also, children use relatively more fat and less carbohydrates than do adolescents or adults. This is another reason why adults should not superimpose adult eating habits on youngsters. During short, intense runs as occur in soccer, children rely more on aerobic energy metabolism in which fat is the major energy source. They do not rely on the anaerobic energy metabolism as do teenagers and adults. This is a distinct difference between very young children and seasoned players.

Because of this, it is important to maintain ample amounts of fat in the diet not only for energy during play, but also for your growth patterns. Keep in mind that fat is a very important source of various vitamins and minerals that are not supplied through other means. The key is to stay away from saturated fats as much as possible since your body requires only small amounts but to load up on the mono and polyunsaturated fats.

Energy problems are compounded even more if your diet is extremely high in carbohydrates (up to 60% or more). By taking in an insufficient amount of fat, especially the good fats which can be utilized for energy, you end up playing hard and fast for only relatively short periods. The increased carbohydrates may be sufficient to fuel intense playing for short periods, but it certainly does not train your body to utilize fats for longer and more intensive play for the entire game. Keep in mind that soccer is a speed-strength sport – not an endurance sport although it too plays a major role especially for halfbacks. Soccer is based mainly on intermittent high intensity activity followed by "slow" activity.

This is the main reason that many players who have high carbohydrate stores at the beginning of play cannot complete a full game going all-out or to play well in the second half or in overtime — they literally run out of gas. The body is unable to utilize more fats or they do not have a sufficient amount of fat for the body to use. You should understand that the body will maintain a minimal amount of fat and cannibalize the muscles before it will use up all the fat in the body. This is why you should have ample muscle and fat stores in the body.

I seriously question the practice of maintaining an extremely high carbohydrate diet or using carbohydrate drinks before playing and during time-outs. By doing this, you rely more and more on sugars for energy instead of utilizing the fats to provide twice the amount of energy. If you eat a more balanced diet and train your body to utilize fats, you may find your playing (and workout) efficiency improving tremendously.

ADJUST YOUR EATING

For more soccer-specific nutritional information, I interviewed Dr. Tobin Watkinson, a renowned clinical nutritionist. He brought out that energy expenditure and nourishment for soccer playing depends to a good extent on whether you are a morning or night person. Because of this you should adjust your eating to meet the demands of the workout or competition.

Time your meals so that if you are more of a morning person, you have your heavier starch, protein and vegetables for breakfast. An omelet would be an excellent food to have. The midmorning snack should include nuts and seeds, proteins which keep your sugars up but don't give you an overabundance. They will run your brain very well.

It is best to have nuts raw and unsalted, unless you will play in very hot weather, at which time a little natural sea salt is good. In addition, have the nuts and seeds alone since they can be digested more easily and efficiently on an empty stomach. When nuts and seeds get cooked with oil they can become rancid (oxidized) and may cause headaches.

If you are an afternoon or evening person and play in the morning, you should start your day with fruit and then have a mid-morning snack of some more substantial protein such as beef jerky. Evening persons need to have the fruits in the morning to raise their blood sugar. If you have some fruit and then a vegetable snack later you will do better.

For an afternoon game the lunch for a morning and afternoon person is basically the same. At lunch do not have only one food item such as pasta or a sandwich. If you have too much protein at lunch, you'll get tired in the afternoon and you'll soon find yourself yawning. Too much starch or too much protein will be converted to sugars making them inappropriate for lunch. An appropriate lunch would be lots of vegetables, and a little protein, such as fish or chicken with some carbohydrates. A morning person should have starch in the morning, and a night person should have starch at night.

Drinking soft drinks or alcohol can be detrimental when working out or playing. The alcohol will dehydrate you and will affect your blood sugar, as will soft drinks and sodas. Any of the sugary soft drinks and fruit juices which you would think would be great are, in fact, not very good. For example, how many oranges does it take to make a glass of orange juice? Not many people would sit down and eat the four or five oranges that it takes to make a glass of unadulterated orange juice. Eating the whole fruit is much better than just having the juice. Also read the labels carefully as many fruit drinks do not contain any fruit juice!

In regard to drinking soda, several studies have shown that teenage girls who drink diet or regular sodas have a much higher risk of bone fracture then those girls who don't and are physically active. Even physically active female soccer players who drink cola beverages have a higher fracture rate than those who don't. One of the reasons for this, is that the girls who choose soft drinks usually don't get enough green vegetables to get ample calcium in their diet which increases their risk for thin, fragile bones that break more easily.

If you are a morning person you should have a snack of some fruit in the afternoon. If you are a night person, you should have the nuts in the middle of the afternoon that the morning person had in the middle of their morning. You need the protein to make it through to your dinner!

After a game or practice, it is relatively easy to compensate for your energy loss merely by consuming ample amounts of food products to give you the same amount of energy but it is extremely difficult to satisfy your energy loss with only food substances such as protein, fats, carbohydrates, and minerals. All these substances are received from food which is a very complex and multi-component chemical system. In regard to food products, the body receives more than 80 different food substances including essential non-synthesized food factors, such as indisposable amino acids, indisposable polyunsaturated fatty acids, vitamins and minerals. From these nutrients, the body synthesizes tens of thousands necessary substances in various combinations for not only the life activity of the body but also for playing soccer.

The problem you face is which essential food substances are the most important for you. The reason for this is that a deficiency of one of these nutrients can lead to insufficient production of hundreds of combinations which are necessary for the body and even a surplus of only one nutrient can interfere with the balance of others. Thus, all serious athletes should receive the necessary balance in the food ration composed of various types of products. The approximate amounts of the daily requirement for athletes vary according to the different sports. For soccer, studies have shown that approximately 1.2 to 1.3 grams of protein per pound of body weight, 1 to 1.2 grams of fat per pound of body weight, 4.8 to 5.2 grams of carbohydrate along with relatively high amounts of vitamin C, the total B-complex, vitamins A and E. In regard to percent of caloric intake, protein should be approximately 17 to 18%, fat 30%, and carbohydrate 52 to 53%.

Most of these figures are for adult players who can expend up to 5,000 to over 6,000 calories a day even at the ages of 11-13. Because of this, youngsters should consume 25 to 30% more calories than non-athletic peers. Some scientists recommend up to 5,000 calories a day for 7 to 12 year old athletes. However, the exact amounts depend to a good extent on your skill level. It is known that the higher your athletic skill, the more economically you burn energy.

Studies done on 14 to 17 year old female soccer players show that they consume approximately 2,500 to 3,000 calories a day. Young athletes especially are distinguished by two nutritional factors – 1) inadequate energy intake, and 2) a nutritionally unbalanced diet. Typically, most youngsters have ample energy intake, but the diets are unbalanced. This is the area that is need of great improvement, and it will show up greatly in your playing ability.

When you get adequate amounts of nutrients, especially proteins, carbohydrates, vitamins and minerals, you will see distinct differences in your play making. If your diet is properly composed and meets the energy needs encountered in game play, you will not only have a greater physical work capacity, but you will be able to recover faster. This is most important as it then enables you to have good practices on the following day or even to compete well on the following day or on the same day when you have multiple games.

Studies have shown that young soccer players are able to increase their work capacity by 15% when their diets are balanced, optimally composed, and high in energy. This includes using some whole food nutritional bars, such as those made by Standard Process, to supply you with ample amounts of energy for a mid-morning or late afternoon snack, especially if you will be playing during the day.

Keep in mind that you are not like your non-athletic peers. How your body handles various nutrients and the foods that you take in are different from those who are relatively inactive. For example, if you consume excess amounts of calcium, sodium, magnesium, and phosphorus, it will not increase your physical work capacity. But when these minerals are taken together in a complex, then there is a strong beneficial effect, especially in regard to the maximum amount of oxygen that you can utilize during play. Non-athletes, on the other hand, do not exhibit this correlation.

An iron deficiency, which leads to anemia reduces your ability to support physical loads as occur in competitive play or practice. Studies have shown that in an intense two-month training period, there are reduced serum iron levels up to 25% in women athletes. The amount of plasma iron, copper and magnesium in the enzyme elements show decreased work capacity. When using supplements containing these elements, work capacity increased significantly.

Vitamin supplementation, especially when the products are made out of natural whole foods, can play several very important roles, especially with young children. Studies done with children beginning at age six and up, show that as the school year progresses, not only does the physical work capacity of the children decrease, but their muscle strength and endurance also decrease. When they take a multivitamin preparation, it has a positive effect on their work capacity. Not only are there substantial increases in muscle endurance, but there are significant increases in muscle strength. These differences start showing up as early as three months after vitamin supplementation.

Taking a vitamin supplement for six months also increases the attention span of six-year old children. There is an appreciable decrease in their fatigue and psycho-emotional strain and there is a rise in their mental and physical activity by the end of the school year. As a result, not only does their school work improve, but also their athletic abilities.

To restore depleted carbohydrates, you should drink a glucose solution during the first six hours after training. It is during this time that glucose is strongly assimilated and is converted into glycogen ready for use by the body during intense play. Many other examples can be given to show the exact role of nutrition on your performance. Suffice it to say that your ability to play hard and play long and well, depends upon properly organized nutrition and on the proper food quality and quantity, which takes into consideration your age and training phase.

KEEPING HYDRATED

According to Dr. Watkinson and other nutritionists, the only thing that can totally rehydrate the cells is water. You can survive on colas, soft drinks, iced tea, or sparkling mineral waters, but they will not rehydrate the cell the way water will. Water is the universal solvent. It enters the cell, re-hydrates it and carries the waste materials away. You will not get these results with other drinks. The reason for this is that the pH in most drinks is inappropriate for the body. When you have a carbonated drink it is acid, versus being alkaline, which is the normal environment to rehydrate the cell.

There are now a lot of designer waters around and many are touted as rehydration drinks. The unfortunate thing about these drinks is that they only contain one or two electrolytes and their major ingredient is some form of sugar. It may taste good at the moment but you will not be feeling very well 20 minutes to an hour later. At this time you may be needing more nutrients, or you will lose your concentration. Best is to have water containing minerals such as calcium, magnesium, potassium and sodium and not be loaded with chemicals.

There are, however, some bottled waters that are proving to be effective in not only quenching your thirst and rehydrating your body but also supplying some needed elements. One such water is OxyWater which has oxygen added to it. The oxygen, once absorbed into the body, enters the blood stream and is then used to help the body in recovery from a workout and in oxidizing some of the waste products. By using oxygenized water as well as natural spring waters, you can get a full complement of needed elements.

Rehydration is especially important to a soccer player and you should drink plenty of water every day. Keep in mind that you are about 80% water and you need to have a continuous supply of good water. Sadly, most of our regular tap water is basically a chemical bath - it is no longer "natural" water. Because of the sweating that you undergo in practice and in play, be sure you maintain your mineral levels, especially sodium. Sea salt is one of the best sources for this needed element.

In regard to fluid and electrolyte requirements, child soccer players produce more metabolic heat per unit of body mass than do adults. This occurs mainly because of the increase in energy expenditure. Because of this, it is important that the extra heat generated be dissipated. If not, the storage of heat in the body may induce heat-related illness. To rid the body of heat, sweat is the best avenue, particularly in hot climates.

However, with excessive sweating, there is also a possibility of greater loss of some electrolytes such as sodium. These are easily replaced at halftime or after the game by adding some natural sea salt to the water in minute amounts or in the food when eating. Most important at this time, is to be drinking sufficient amounts of water, especially good, clean water that is not loaded with chemicals. A lack of water can limit playing ability much more than any loss of electrolytes. Also, a lack of salt in the body can lead to muscle cramps. Using ample amounts of natural sea salt can help prevent this.

Trained athletes, when acclimated to heat, produce much more sweat than do non-athletes. Because of this, their fluid replacement requirements are considerably higher. This is why it is important that you learn to drink more water. Since flavor of the drinking water is very important, be sure that it is good, clean water so that it has a good taste. In many areas, tap water does not taste very good because of all the added chemicals, and you will not drink much. You should drink clean water or use waters such as OxyWater to provide even extra benefits while helping to hydrate you.

One way to determine if you are getting enough water, is to weigh yourself before and after a training session or after a major game. When there are major changes in body weight, it is usually due to loss of body fluid content. If you do not drink enough water to restore your normal body weight between practices or competitions, it will show up in the weighing. This will indicate the need for more water. However, do not rely on this method to replace your water supply since the differences relate more to major discrepancies in water supply.

Cooling a drink to refrigerator temperature may make water more palatable but there are varying opinions as to how cold consumed water should be, especially when the body is hot. I typically recommend drinking water that is cool, but not cold. Hot water does not taste good, therefore, cooling is necessary. But when water is too cold, it is very hard to drink sufficient amounts and the extreme cold can "shock" the body unfavorably. Therefore, cool water appears to be the best. Adding a small amount of natural sea salt to the water, but not to the point where it creates a salty flavor, will further stimulate your thirst and increase the amount of fluid that you can take in.

CONCENTRATION

Soccer players, especially those who play a lot, need to maintain their concentration throughout the game and especially near the end of the game. Concentration is basically brain chemistry, i.e., a balance between your ability to utilize the fuel that you have taken in and your ability to convert it into the appropriate brain chemistries. All the amino acids, which are the small building blocks of proteins, are the precursors to building the brain chemistries we hear so much about today. This includes serotonin, melatonin, epinephrine, and norepinephrine as well as the other products that our brains need to be able to function well.

If you are exercising or playing and are under stress, you are going to use a higher amount of your brain fuels. If you are unable to replenish these fuels due to the burning up of the raw material or not having adequate raw material, your body will "stall out." If you have a high demand, as for example, when you are in an important competitive game and your body is unable to have the appropriate fuels to do what is needed, then you will be unable to concentrate.

Emotional needs require even more nutritional support. For example, when there is a heavy emotional component (as when you are playing in a league or championship game), you can burn up to 25 percent more calories than in regular play or in practice. This is why it is so important to be well fortified nutritionally. Keep in mind that the minimum standards established for various vitamins and minerals are for sedentary people – not athletes. You need more than the average person!

CONCLUSION

Be sure to have a wide range of foods and to follow the guidelines that have been discussed. This means having ample amounts of vegetables, meats, breads, nuts, seeds and some fruit in order to get a full range of these very rich sources of all vitamins and minerals. Unfortunately, many people today are taking synthetic and incomplete vitamins that create vitamin deficiencies which cause some of the mental fogs that people get into at times. We are not as smart as nature in our ability to produce a nutrient that is as complete as what nature can produce.

When you eat wholesome, organic foods, you get a complete source of the nutrients that are needed. Chemical vitamins need the necessary co-factors to be able to complete their activity. If there is something that they are deficient in, the chemical vitamins will steal your body stores of the particular vitamin or mineral to become complete. Thus, after you take chemical (synthetic) vitamins, many times the end result is that you may be more deficient than you were before you took them! You should strive to have a full complement of natural food vitamins and minerals and to use whole food supplements such as those produced by Standard Process. They are the same as eating whole organic foods.

10

Designing Your Exercise Program

Before setting up a program specific to you, it is necessary to consider several factors that may influence your decision in regard to the time and energy expended. For example, how much time should you devote to strength development in an overall training program? The time factor is a major objection that many players and coaches have against a separate strength development program. As a result, they often integrate strength training with soccer drills and run up hills or stairs. These programs are effective but they do not fulfill the goals of special strength training.

Soccer drills and stair running lack a key element, progressive overload. This means that you cannot regulate the intensity of the loads so that the muscles can respond with continual increases in strength. For example, merely running stairs, which is not even specific to soccer skills and which can teach you bad habits, does not lead to greater levels of strength except when first starting this exercise. The more you run up and down, the more you develop muscular endurance, not strength or explosiveness.

As brought out in my research, strength and endurance are related and are on a continuum. In the initial stages of training both strength and endurance are developed simultaneously. However, they are both very specific physical qualities and require separate training programs. There is no single type of exercise that is capable of simultaneously developing both of these qualities (or others) to the level needed in soccer.

As important as strength increases are, the main objective is to play better, not to become the strongest woman on the team. You have only so much time and energy to train. Because of this, strength development which is based on your needs and the requirements of the game, should be placed in its proper perspective in the overall training program. Since speed and quickness are so important in high-level play, it should be the focus of your strength and explosive training.

Specific strength is developed through specific adaptation to the demands you place on the muscle. Thus, the loading must be carried out in a progressive manner in order to constantly raise the level of strength. This is best done through the use of cable weights, rubber tubing, and free weights (dumbbells and barbells). These types of equipment are most effective for the development of strength for soccer players and the total energy output is minimal when compared to stair climbing or playing itself. It can improve your playing without playing! Weather conditions do not prohibit their use and the resistance can be adjusted to your abilities.

Weight (resistance) training can be done at home with adjustable weights and rubber tubing. The advantages of using such equipment are:

1. The overload principle can be made progressive by the gradual increase of the resistance used, thereby assuring a continuity of strength gains in the muscles involved in running and cutting.

2. Resistance training can be used to develop strength in any or all of the muscles of the body according to your requirements. For example, strength of the hip flexors which is highly specific to a player in running and in taking a quick first step, can best be developed to the optimal level through the use of the thigh drive exercise with progressive resistance increases. It is best done with rubber tubing or on a pulley cable.

3. The strength development program can be designed primarily to develop strength in those muscles which assist you in sprinting and cutting.

For your running and cutting exercise program to be most effective, you must individualize it according to whether you are a recreational or competitive player and the position you play. In addition, the amount of resistance that you use, the kind and number of exercises that you execute, and the number of sets and repetitions used for each exercise depend on your mastery of the exercises and your mastery of the game skills. Keep in mind that as your levels of strength, speed and quickness improve, you must move up to the next level of difficulty.

GETTING STARTED

For beginners and those who have not worked out for many months or more, it is necessary to first go through a learning and familiarization stage to gradually accustom your body to exercise. To help prevent soreness or discomfort, read (and sometimes re-read) exactly how to do the exercises and how to make progress. Have this book with you when you train.

LEARNING, MODIFYING AND PERFECTING YOUR RUNNING AND CUTTING TECHNIQUE

To make your technique (skill) work most effective, it is important that you follow several very important guidelines:

1. Always be in an energetic and alert state of mind when practicing. It is important to understand that all soccer skills are neuromuscular skills. They require active involvement of the nervous system together with the muscular system. Thus, the nerves and muscles must have high energy levels in order to carry out the necessary movements with precision. This is why technique work is always done first in the training session or done separately at another time of day, when you are not in a fatigue state.

2. Do not repeat one action for an excessively long period of time. Do the movement until you feel that you can no longer do it as well or in the same movement pattern. Always stop at the first signs of fatigue so that you do not develop a different neuromuscular pathway for execution of the skill. You must learn the most effective technique one way and reinforce it in the same way until it becomes automatic. Your body will automatically make the necessary changes when you are in a fatigue state to still ensure effective execution of the skill. Do not learn the skill when you are in a fatigue state! You will be very erratic and you will not achieve the necessary mastery of the action to ensure greater speed and quickness.

3. Keep your practice sessions relatively short. When working on cutting technique it is important that you concentrate on the movements being executed. After 20-30 repetitions you have probably accomplished as much as possible in relation to making the changes needed. Then switch to a different skill or joint action. Keep in mind that working on technique involves total mental concentration as well as full body energy in order to carry out the actions that are needed.

4. Follow the technique work with specialized strength exercises to more strongly reinforce the specific joint actions. For example, when working on the knee drive action to improve the quickness of your first step or running speed, do the knee drive strength

exercise in the same way on every repetition to reinforce the feel of driving the knee forward. In this way you can enhance the technique execution together with additional strength. Execution of a special strength exercise takes maximum concentration in order to develop the correct movement pathway and the muscle feel needed to be able to duplicate the action every time during play.

MODIFYING AND PERFECTING YOUR PHYSICAL ABILITIES

Do one exercise for 3-5 repetitions with light resistance. When using rubber tubing, adjust the length so that you can execute the exercise easily through a full ROM. This means that you do the exercise (up and down or away and back) 3-4 times. Execute each repetition at a moderate rate of speed.

As you do the exercise, concentrate on exactly how you are doing it and how it feels. Recognize what each exercise feels like and which muscles are working. In this way you will gain a better feel for the movement and how it relates to cutting and running. After completing 3-5 repetitions, relax and then get ready for the next exercise. Read the description and then do several repetitions. Proceed in this manner until you do all the exercises selected.

You do not have to do every exercise that is described in this book for each joint action. When first beginning, pick out exercises for your troublesome areas or the actions you would like to improve. Other exercises can be attempted the following week or as you get used to doing the core (for you) exercises. For example, a sample strength exercise program may include the following exercises:
1. Good morning
2. Back raise
3. Knee drive
4. Heel raise
5. Squat
6. Reverse trunk twist
7. Reverse sit up

If you desire greater improvement of particular actions include even more exercises. However, for most players, this sample program is quite sufficient for the first 2 to 6 weeks, especially in regard to learning the exercises. It is important that you record each exercise and the number of repetitions done so that you know exactly where you are on each exercise at the next workout.

PERSONALIZE YOUR PROGRAM

Each of you is a unique individual and you will respond to the exercises differently. This is why you should never copy what someone else is doing. Because someone you know may have responded quickly to the exercises, it does not mean that your body will also respond in the same manner. Each of you has her own rate and amount of development possible.

If you copy someone else's program regardless of how successful it is, you take a chance of getting injured. Not only may the resistance be greater than what your muscles and joints can handle, but the way the exercise is executed by another person may not fit the way your body is designed to move. In these instances there is a high likelihood of injury. Your program must be individualized, just as your playing ability is very individual. You must develop your physical abilities in tandem with your skill (technique) execution.

WHEN TO WORK OUT

Schedule your strength exercise workouts so that they are not done immediately before or after your soccer practice or play. An ideal situation would be to do the exercises in the morning and to play (or practice) in the afternoon. If you prefer playing in the morning then you should do the exercises in late afternoon or evening. The key here is to give yourself a few hours of rest and recovery in between. Do the exercises consistently and at a fairly regular time so that you have ample time for recovery and for your body to adapt to the exercises.

REPETITIONS AND SETS

Keep adding one or two repetitions at each workout (or each week) until you reach 15-20 repetitions maximum (RM). This means you cannot do any more repetitions with the resistance selected. When you repeatedly reach 20 RM (or slightly more) you will be ready to increase the resistance for that particular exercise. If you have not reached 20 RM in the other exercises remain on the same level.

After a few weeks you will become more comfortable with the exercises and have greater confidence. Since you will be able to handle more resistance and execute more repetitions without any discomfort or trepidation, you may want to add other exercises at this time. If you experience soreness on any workout day or on the day after, it means you did too many repetitions or used too much resistance. When this happens, use the same or even less resistance in the next workout to help your body recover. Gradually increase the resistance or repetitions as you feel up to it. To aid in your recovery and to help prevent soreness, many players have found the use of OxyWater® (oxygenized water) and Velvet Antler, respectively, to be especially effective.

At this time you should do only one set of each exercise. A set means doing a particular number of repetitions of one exercise one time. For example, if you do 20 RM of the squat this constitutes one set of the exercise. If you then do an additional 20 RM or less, it is considered set number two.

Since the main purpose of the workout program at this time is to familiarize you with the exercises and to gradually have your body adapt to the exercises and the workout, only one set is needed. Doing more than one set will not produce greater increases in strength. A greater number of sets is needed only when you need greater gains after you become more fit and have better mastery of the exercises. This is when additional sets play their most important role.

DAYS PER WEEK

For technique learning and improvement, you should practice for short periods, 5-6 days per week. For strength, you should work out three days per week with each session lasting a maximum of 30-45 minutes. For a minimum of 90 minutes a week, you can gain sufficient strength and flexibility to enable you to run and cut faster. This is especially true of players who have never strength trained. Higher level players usually require more time because of the need for not only strength but speed-strength training.

You will reach 15-20 RM fairly rapidly in some exercises while in other exercises progress may be slower. This is perfectly normal since some muscles take longer to respond and certain exercises are easier to learn than others. For some women it may take 1-2 months to reach 15-20 RM in all the exercises.

It is important that you work out on a regular basis. When on a 3 days per week program you must not skip days and say, "I will do four days next week because I only did two this week." This is not effective. Working out more than three days per week does not bring additional benefits, and can lead to overtraining and the possibility of injury and soreness. A three day a week program allows for a day's rest in between to give your muscles ample time to fully recover. As a result, it will not interfere with your playing! When you are more fit, working out 4-6 times per week can be successfully integrated with your playing.

To get maximum benefit from the strength training program, you should continue playing to constantly make minor adjustments in how you execute the running and cutting actions. Most of the changes will be made unconsciously because of the muscular feel developed when doing the exercises. The changes will feel very natural to you! However, you should not be doing all-out sprints or cuts at this time. Not only may it lead to injury but it does not allow you to concentrate on your form or technique changes. Once technique is mastered, gradually increase the speed of execution until it duplicates what takes place in game play.

INCREASING THE DIFFICULTY

When you reach 15-20 RM for each exercise, and the exercises become "easy", you will be ready to make changes. At this time the workouts become more strenuous. If you are already strong and have been working out regularly, you can begin on this level, especially if you are already familiar with the exercises. However, when starting a new exercise, start as previously described and gradually build up to the level needed.

Regardless of whether you use the Active Cords (rubber tubing), dumbbells or barbells, when you reach about 20 RM or more regularly, increase the resistance. Doing this should bring you down to 12-15 RM. Then work back up to 20 RM and repeat the process. When you do an exercise for 15-20 RM it is important that the last repetition be the most that you can do with proper technique. Do not, for example, do 15 or 20 repetitions and still feel refreshed. When you finish the set you should feel slightly out of breath and have muscular fatigue.

Be in tune with your body as you do the exercises. Only in this way can you find out what is working for you and which exercises appear to be most effective. You can then make the necessary changes in the exercises or exercise program to produce the desired results. If you need more work on certain muscles or movements, add another set of selected exercises.

MAKING THE WORKOUT MORE SPECIFIC

You can change how well you play significantly, depending not only on which exercises you use, but also on how many repetitions and sets you use. Thus, how you set up your program at this time is critical to your success. Most important is that you make your workout specific not only to your position but to the changes you desire. For example, fullbacks need to be able to execute quick bursts of maximum speed. Midfielders need to be able to do this and to maintain longer top speed runs.

Keep in mind that your workout program for strength is different from what it will be for producing increases in speed-strength. In essence, the workouts must be geared toward the qualities you are desirous of improving as well as the role that they play in your particular position.

For example, beginners may find great improvement in their performance from doing only one set of 15-20 RM. The strength gains at this time will raise the level of neuromuscular coordination and muscular and cardiovascular endurance which play equally important roles. A more advanced player needs greater levels of speed-strength, starting strength, and explosive strength. Thus the programs for different levels of players must be different, yet include some of the same exercises.

DEVELOPING GREATER STRENGTH

To increase strength after the basic training you should do 2-3 sets of the key specific exercises. Using greater resistance at this time (which is needed for greater strength) requires warm-up or initial preparation of the muscles. Thus, for the first set (when doing three or more sets), do 10 repetitions with half the resistance that you will be using in set two. In set two, do 8-10 RM for strength. Follow this with another set of 8-10 RM if more strength is needed and then do set three (or four) in which you do 15 RM for muscular endurance.

After you do the first set, rest for approximately 30 to 60 seconds for recovery. (Longer, if doing explosive strength exercises.) Then repeat the same exercise for the second set. You can also do another exercise for different muscles in between sets so that you can do more exercises in a shorter amount of time. If you have a very intense program, as is often needed with high level players, a split program may be beneficial. This means that you do the upper and lower body exercises twice a week on alternate days with two days of rest for each. For example, Monday and Thursday - upper body; Tuesday and Friday - lower body; Wednesday and Saturday - special workouts for other qualities such as flexibility, agility, coordination, etc.

Completing 3-4 sets, a set for warm-up, 1-2 sets for strength, and a set for endurance, is usually sufficient for most players at this time. Most important is that you do the key special exercises to not only improve your weak actions but to enhance your strong points. All your exercises should be specific to your running and cutting actions in need of improvement (after your base conditioning).

There is no need for very great resistance in this program. Keep in mind that if you use too much resistance, your ROM will decrease which, in turn can negatively affect your playing. Thus, be sure that you do the exercises exactly as described regardless of how many sets and repetitions you do.

SPEED-STRENGTH AND EXPLOSIVE TRAINING

Strength coupled with speed is most important for all players, but especially for more advanced players. Speed-strength and explosive training is the key to increasing speed and quickness. However, such training should be done only after you have a well established strength base. Some forms of explosive training such as introductory plyometrics can be done without a high level strength base. These workouts are not intense and consist mainly of easy jump exercises. If you do strength training three times a week, introductory speed-strength work is done on the alternate days but no more than twice a week (three times a week if the workouts are easy).

The introduction of speed-strength work should be slow and gradual. It should begin with easy preparatory type jump exercises as well as combinations of strength and explosive movements. For example, holding a squat position with resistance for up to 4-5 seconds and then exploding upward. To ensure that you introduce the explosive work slowly and gradually, you should begin with activities such as simple skipping, hopping, jumping, leaping and bounding. These activities prepare the muscles for more intense work later.

If you are on a four-day split program, the speed-strength work can be sequenced with the strength training. In this case, the speed-strength work is done first (after a vigorous warm-up) and the workout is ended with strength and in some cases endurance work. Depending upon your level of fitness and mastery of the exercises, the gradual build up should last anywhere from four to eight or more weeks.

When you are capable of correctly doing high intensity jumps you will be ready for a maximum intensity workout. At this time you should gradually increase the number of exercises that are done explosively. Begin with only a few exercises and then build up the number of exercises and/or the number of sets done for each exercise. Be sure that you do each exercise correctly to not only get maximum benefits from the work, but to prevent injury.

Beginners and young players aged 6-12 should use speed-strength and explosive training sparingly. Keep in mind that initially, aerobic capabilities and strength are most important. Thus up to 80% of the training should be devoted to improvement of the aerobic capabilities and muscular strength and endurance. Speed work should comprise about 20% of the workouts. Older beginners can do three to four speed-strength or lead-up plyometric exercises for one to two sets in the training session. These exercises should precede the strength or endurance training.

The intensity of the work when doing speed-strength and explosive training for advanced players (late teens and older) is very high. Because of this, more rest is needed in between sets, making the workouts at this time longer. The total workout can last up to two hours especially if it includes special strength training.

Speed-strength and explosive training should be done only in the specialized period of training (after general conditioning and before competition). Because this type of training has a strong residual effect, you should stop such training at least one-two weeks before competition. This is needed to give the muscles ample time to fully adapt and to be ready for all out performance during competition.

SPEED TRAINING

Speed and quickness training which consists mainly of all-out sprints, explosive strength exercises and explosive agility (cutting) exercises should be done no more than two times a week (except when learning technique). When sprinting, it is important to maintain good running technique. When fatigue sets in your technique changes and you will develop different neuromuscular pathways. However, when the nervous system is fresh you can duplicate exactly the correct technique to ensure the fastest running and cutting. Because of this, speed and quickness work should always precede other types of training.

The same holds true for explosive work. You should have ample rest in between exercises or sets so that the muscles are capable of a maximal contraction when doing the most intense forms of explosive training. Explosive exercises should never be done when you are in a fatigue state.

If you are in the process of changing or modifying your running or cutting technique it is important that you not do all-out speed training. Once you master the necessary technique you can then gradually increase speed and quickness while still maintaining good technique. If you do all-out agility exercises or speed running when trying to modify technique, you will inadvertently go back to your old form which will greatly interfere with any changes you are trying to make.

Do not do all-out speed training when you are also doing heavy weight training. The two are not compatible. The very intense strength training should be decreasing and speed-strength training increasing as you begin to introduce all-out speed training. Speed work, which usually consists of various sprints and speed and explosive skills, is best done when you have already completed the strength training phase and are moving into the phase of speed and explosive training. In this situation the explosive exercises better prepare the muscles for all-out running and cutting.

Over-speed training can also be done at this time. When doing over-speed training, you actually run faster than you can volitionally. The over-speed teaches the nervous and muscular systems what it is like to experience faster and quicker movements. There are various ways of achieving speed overload and the application of each method must be quite precise. For example, in downhill running, the distance must not be very great and the angle of the slope must be within certain limits. Running with a parachute or jumping and running with extra weight can be effective; but how much weight and where it is distributed on the body play extremely important roles.

Because each of these methods requires considerable detail and great precision, they are not discussed in detail in this book. Note, however that it is easy to overdo such training and to misinterpret how the training should be done. For this reason it is purposely omitted here in an aim to prevent injury. If you feel you are ready for such training (especially if you are a high level player), contact Sports Training, Inc., or Dr. Yessis for additional information.

Also purposefully omitted are the exact number of sets, reps and amount of weight that you should use in the different periods of training. The reason for this is that all players are different in their physical abilities, and thus, the programs for each player should be different. Merely because you are on a Division I team does not mean that you are physically more capable than someone on a Division III team. In fact, it can be just the opposite. Thus, the programs for strength and other physical qualities do not necessarily depend upon the division or type of player you are, but solely on your physical abilities and mastery of the skills.

Coaches have a tendency to have all players do the same workouts mainly for efficiency and convenience, not for maximum effectiveness. To maximize each player's program requires individualized work which takes more time and effort. Thus, the burden should not rest solely on the shoulders of the coach; it must also be your responsibility. Only you can do the work and if you are serious about your playing and want to improve to your maximum then it behooves you to take a very strong interest in determining what your abilities are and how they can be improved. You cannot rely only on the coach.

Also keep in mind that there are many coaches who are not competent in technique and physical training and, thus, do very little in these areas to improve your performance. They are usually great strategists, know how to get good team work from the players and how to play you against other teams. Conditioning and preparing you physically for the tasks involved in soccer as well as improving your movement skills are typically beyond most coaches, including strength coaches. Keep in mind that such training has typically been ignored in the curriculum for these coaches. It is only in recent years that improved technique is being recognized as indispensable to improved performances.

Establishing your own individualized training program is not very difficult. If you have come this far in the book you should already have a good understanding of what is involved in improving your performance. Many guidelines on how you should construct your program, which exercises you should include and how many sets and reps should be done, have been presented. This should give you enough information to begin developing your training program. If you keep a diary you will know exactly what you are doing and will be able to make adjustments as you move along. Do not rely on others to do the training for you. You must be actively involved in the process in order to make it most effective.

INTEGRATED TRAINING

Soccer players must work on more than simply improving one quality, as for example, speed. You must do separate training for strength, flexibility, neuromuscular coordination (technique), speed- strength (power), muscular strength, cardiovascular endurance and so on. How to integrate these different workouts into one or more training sessions thus becomes very important, especially in view of the limited time that you may have. In general, following is the order in which the different physical qualities should be worked on in one session.

1.Technique (Skill) Learning:

In order to most effectively learn new technique or to modify technique, your nervous system must be in a high energy state. In essence, you must be alert to and aware of exactly what you are doing. You must be tuned into the feedback you receive and capable of making the changes needed to improve the actions desired. Because of this, technique must be first in your training before you do much physical work. Note that this is predicated on the fact that you have already developed base levels of strength and endurance.

2. Speed and Explosive Training

If no technique work is done, speed and explosive training move to the number one position. However, before undertaking such work it is important that you have an adequate warm-up to prepare the muscles for the high intensity encountered. If you wish to do both technique and speed work in the same session, the amount of technique work should be minimal. It should be used mainly for reinforcement of particular coordinations and as a warm-up to the speed and explosive training.

3. Specialized Strength Work

All strength exercises that duplicate particular aspects of your running and cutting technique must be done prior to other types of strength training. At this time you must be relatively fresh and energetic so that you can concentrate on developing the muscular feel of the movements. Thus, it follows speed and explosive work but only if you are not in a fatigue state.

4. General All-round Strength Training

Training that is general, such as all-round conditioning, and which is not specific to the joint actions involved in specific soccer skills can be done when in a fatigue state. Because of this it follows the other types of training that require maximum levels of energy. This type of training is often done after practice.

5. Muscular Endurance/Cardiovascular Endurance

Usually these two qualities are combined but they can also be done separately. For example, there are instances when you must work on muscular endurance as needed in a typical game. Such workouts are localized to particular joint actions. Cardiovascular work may automatically be included if it involves large body parts.

In cardiovascular work the total body is usually involved, as for example, long distance or cross-country running, cycling and rowing. Endurance should always be the last type of training done in the session. It should never be used as a warm-up. Light jogging in which the heart rate stays well below the training zone is acceptable for warm up and recovery. But to have a training effect in endurance work, you must have the heartbeat in the range where it will produce results.

For example, for relatively young 17-35 year-old athletes, to produce an aerobic training effect, the heart rate (HR) should be in the range of 140-160 beats per minute (B/M). For a combination training effect of aerobic and anaerobic capabilities the HR should be 160-180 B/M. To develop the anaerobic system the HR should be in the upper range of 180-200 B/M. Once you have your base aerobic system developed, you should strive to run as close as possible to your anaerobic threshold, i.e., about 155-160 bpm so that you become more efficient at burning fats for your fuel and to be able to run faster for longer distances and overall duration.

MAINTAINING SPEED, STRENGTH AND ENDURANCE

It is not necessary to continually increase your strength or muscular endurance. This is especially true if you are a recreational player. At this time maintaining your developed strength or endurance levels is most important. Keep in mind that if you cease your workouts and only play, you'll lose some of the gained strength and endurance. This, in turn, will affect not only your speed and quickness, but also your technique, which may then lead to injury.

Continual increases in strength and other physical qualities are not called for in-season (competitive season). In-season, maintaining and perfecting your skill and the development of strategy based on your physical and technical abilities, becomes most important for winning success. All major increases in your physical abilities and technique changes should take place prior to the season.

In season, to improve performance, you should continue to do speed and quickness work. In addition, explosive cutting and running and other forms of speed-strength work are done to bring about even greater gains in speed and quickness. However, because of the amount of speed and quickness work done, the amount of strength training is decreased and in many cases, stopped to prevent injury. The speed and explosive training should maintain the achieved strength levels. If not, maintenance work should be incorporated.

For most recreational players, once a level of strength and endurance is attained that enables you to play well, maintaining your speed-strength and endurance is all that is called for. If you want to become faster or quicker, then you should increase your levels of speed-strength.

To maintain your levels of strength and endurance, you should continue to work out 1-2 days per week and do one set of the key exercises. In some cases two sets may be needed in certain exercises. The exact number of repetitions and sets will depend on your level of fitness and your goals. For most players, one set for 10-20 RM is sufficient when done twice a week. Advanced players may require more work to maintain speed and quickness especially if the speed and explosive work or playing is not sufficient to maintain achieved strength levels.

If you stop your training and only play, you may find your skill execution changing. This is especially true as you age. But by maintaining your strength and flexibility levels, you will be able to maintain the ability to play basically the same way in the later years as in your youth. Increase your physical abilities and you will play on a higher skill level.

PRINCIPLES OF TRAINING

Working out can mean many things to different people, but how you work out is critical to your development. To get the maximum results, you should adhere to the following principles of exercise:

INDIVIDUALIZATION

You are a unique individual. Aside from the obvious structural differences there are also physiological differences in the muscular, circulatory and nervous systems that require differences in your program. This is why you must be the one to make the final decision as to exactly which and how many exercises are needed and how many sets and reps should be done. Your training program should be for you and only you.

Even though you cannot change your genetic make-up (which only determines one third of your potential), you can greatly modify your speed, strength, flexibility and other qualities. I have worked with many players who have literally transformed their bodies and their playing abilities. Some started off being fairly lackadaisical but ended up being extremely active exercisers.

GRADUALNESS

Regardless of your exercise program or level of performance, any increases in speed, flexibility, strength, resistance, repetitions or sets should be very gradual. For example, if you are accustomed to doing 15 RM for two sets, you should not in one day change to 50 or 60 repetitions or do four sets. Your body is not ready for such abrupt changes and because of this injuries may occur. To prevent injury and to maximize your results, all gains should be gradual.

PROGRESSIVENESS

In order to continually show increases in speed, muscular strength and endurance, you must progressively but gradually increase the amount of resistance (intensity), the number of exercises or the total number of repetitions (volume) used. If you continue working at the same level and do the same number of exercises, sets and reps you will only maintain your achieved fitness level.

OVERLOAD

Overload means that you do more than what your body is accustomed to. In order to develop greater strength you must use additional resistance. To increase flexibility you must increase the range of motion. Other ways to achieve overload include increasing the rate of work, i.e., doing the exercises at a slightly faster rate of speed or in an explosive manner. These methods, however, apply more to advanced players and should be used only after you have achieved base levels of strength and endurance.

AWARENESS

The principle of awareness is very important. To be aware you should keep a record of your workouts. Record not only the resistance, sets and repetitions for each exercise, but also how you feel. Make notations of what you experience, both mentally and physically.

This is especially important for those of you who respond differently in each phase of the menstrual cycle. Some women do their best work (or playing) after menstruation, while others perform better at the actual time of menstruation. Because of this you should determine when you can do your most productive work and schedule the workouts around the menstrual cycle. In general, stay away from very strenuous activity (such as using heavy resistance) during the menstrual period.

Awareness also means being cognizant of what is happening to your body. You should learn what each exercise feels like and how your body responds to it. In time, you develop a muscle memory so that when you execute the exercise (or skill technique) you can tell immediately if it is working for you or if something is amiss. When things do not feel right, you should check to see if your execution is correct or if there is some other problem that is interfering.

CONSISTENCY

Without consistency in your exercise program, all the work that you do may come to naught. For example, after each workout your energy supply is used up. It is replaced while you are resting and sleeping when additional energy supplies for later use are deposited. This is known as supercompensation. If you do not exercise sufficiently to use this extra energy that has been deposited, the body will re-absorb it and as a result you may be left with the same energy as before. For example, I am sure you have noticed that when you have not played or worked out for a while or have become sedentary you actually become more tired than if you were active throughout the entire day.

Consistency, which means doing the exercises on a regular basis, is the key to success in any exercise or training program. What I recommend, therefore, is that you block off the time needed in your busy schedule so that the exercise program becomes as important as your other activities.

If for some reason you are unable to work out for a week or two, start your exercises again upon your return using less resistance. In one or two days you should get back into the groove of doing the exercises and seeing results. Do not be overly concerned when situations arise that do not allow you to continue on the program since they can be made up. However, do not allow this to happen on a regular basis.

If you want to improve your playing most effectively and in the shortest amount of time, schedule the exercises you should do. Once you set up a regular exercise program you will see the benefits quite soon. It is at this time that you will become hooked. You will look forward to doing the exercises because you will see what the exercises are doing for you and how they are improving your skill execution and overall playing. You will also experience greater confidence in yourself, which will show up in better playing and in everyday life.

PERIODIZATION

To assist you in how the workouts should be distributed throughout the year, it is important to understand the concept of periodization and cycling. In periodization, the year is divided into different periods, or phases of training. In each phase you train in a specific manner to gain certain physical qualities or attain certain results. The development you achieve enables you to do the training called for in the next period of training. The positive changes you experience from each period of training make it possible for you to tackle the next phase of training which eventually leads to your ultimate goal.

The periods of training and the types of training done in each period must vary. Soccer players have multiple objectives – not only must you increase strength to improve your abilities but you must also increase speed-strength, explosiveness, speed, coordination and cardiovascular and respiratory endurance. Thus your training has several directions and is divided between technique, strength, flexibility, various aspects of speed-strength (explosive) and endurance training. In many cases, these objectives are accomplished while still playing competitively.

However, it becomes increasingly difficult to maintain an effective supplementary training program if you are on a competitive schedule year-round. When you are constantly playing, it becomes very difficult to prepare yourself for the best playing. Remember that only playing is not the most effective way to increase your speed and quickness. Nor is it the best way to improve your kicking ability, except possibly for accuracy. Because of this, it is strongly recommended that you select the particular competitive period that is most important or matches that are most important. Then, set up a training program around the most important events. In essence, you will train through certain competitive periods. The competition in this case, will be used as a training session. You still play your best, but it may not be the best that you are capable of if you trained specifically for the game or event.

THE PERIODIZATION PLAN

In soccer there is one major scholastic competitive season. Some players also play in outside leagues and often on a year-round basis. Because of this, some of the competition should be considered as training sessions rather than major competitive sessions that require specialized training for preparation. The competition season also varies depending on where you live. When team practices begin, you usually have only one to two months to prepare for the season. This is inadequate if you truly expect to improve your game appreciably. Keep in mind that league practice and competitive schedules are not set up to provide an ideal situation for improving your talents. Because of this it is up to you to adequately prepare yourself to play your best when the major season arrives. Thus, follow the following yearly program as best as possible.

PHASE ONE - GENERAL PHYSICAL PREPARATION

The initial stage of training consists of general preparatory or general conditioning exercises to strengthen all the major muscles and joints. Some specialized strength exercises may also be included. This should prepare you for the more intense training to follow. This period is also used for rehabilitation of injured muscles and joints and strengthening or bringing the lagging muscles up to par. The work in this period is very general in nature so that psychological stress does not build up. You accustom your body to working out with different exercises and activities. The volume of work done is very high but the intensity is low. In essence, you use this period to prepare your body for future training. This is the getting started period which may also include low-level playing practice.

The exact length of time spent in this phase depends upon your level of mastery of the exercises, mastery of the soccer skills, your level of fitness, age and so on. The younger or more novice you are, the more time you should spend in this phase of training in order to increase strength, endurance and other physical qualities. Thus, for beginners, this phase can last up to three-four months.

If you are a high-level player you can spend up to two to four weeks in this period mainly to bring the body up to a level that will enable you to do more intense training. This is based on the assumption that you remain in good physical condition and that you have maintained your skills throughout the year. On this level you do not lose your sports form from the previous year. For most players, this period lasts approximately six to eight weeks.

The general all-around strength program should include many varied strength exercises especially for the lower body. Exercises that can be included are the heel raise, toe raise, squat, hip abduction, hip flexion, hip extension, good morning, and glute-ham-gastroc raise. These lower body exercises develop the leg and hip muscles in the different actions which are most important in movement on the field.

Midsection exercises include the reverse sit-up, reverse trunk twist and back raise. These exercises play a very important role not only in strengthening the back to help prevent injury, but in developing a muscular corset around the midsection. A strong midsection is needed to transfer the forces from the legs to the upper body in jumping and for powerful sprinting and cutting. In addition, development of the midsection muscles, especially the rotational muscles, are extremely important in executing feints, and different cutting actions. They are the key to enhancing your ability to tackle the ball and to quickly reach out to break up a play or shot. Upper body exercises can vary greatly but should include exercises for the chest, back and arms.

Doing such strength exercises is very beneficial since they involve all of the major and many of the minor muscles involved in a multitude of movements. They prepare your body for more intense weight training exercises and for executing soccer skills more effectively. Some of these exercises can be used for rehabilitation purposes while some can be used to strengthen muscles that have been weakened because of injury or overuse in particular movements.

You do not have to do every exercise. You should first determine your strong and weak points and then do exercises to bring up your weak points so that you are more balanced in your overall development. However, do not neglect the strong points; they must still be improved. But, the amount of work done on your strong points at this time should be less than what you do for the weaker or lagging aspects of your muscle strength.

PHASE TWO – SPECIALIZED PHYSICAL TRAINING

The specialized physical training period begins gradually as the general preparatory period comes to an end. This way there is a smooth transition from the general to specific training.

In specialized physical training, the work becomes very specific to running and cutting (and other soccer skills). This means practicing the specific game skills and doing specific exercises for increasing strength, speed-strength and endurance exactly as used in competition. The exercises also duplicate the same range of motion and type of muscular contraction. Thus the exercises enhance specific skill execution.

Your exact workout at this time depends upon your level of ability and stage of training. A sample program can consist of some of the following exercises which are explained in detail in the previous chapters.

To improve cutting actions:
- Explosive side jumps
- Single leg side, forward and backward jumps
- Hip abduction
- Lunge
- Side lunge
- Ankle abduction
- Knee extensions

For improved running speed and a quick first step:
- Jumps out of a squat
- Plyometric (explosive) exercises
- Quick movements out of the athletic stance
- Lunge
- The knee drive
- Pawback
- Ankle extensions

More advanced or high level players may have a similar program but they usually include more sets of the explosive exercises or use a split program to do both lower body, midsection and total body explosive exercises together with specialized strength exercises to enhance particular actions. Thus a sample program may look as follows:

Monday and Thursday
To improve cutting ability:
- Explosive double leg side jumps
- Explosive single leg side jumps
- Split-squat jumps with weights in the hands or with the pull of rubber tubing
- Four-way floor jumps

Each of these exercises are done for 2-3 sets of 10.

These explosive exercises are then followed with lower body strength exercises. This may include squats, heel raises, standing knee extensions, glute-ham-gastroc raises, back raises, hip extensions, hip abductions and lunges.

Tuesday and Friday
To improve running speed:
- 10-yard sprints
- 30-yard sprints
- Ankle jumps
- Explosive thigh drive
- Standing starts
- Explosive heel raises
- Single leg jumps for height and distance

These explosive exercises are then followed with special strength exercises. For example, knee drive, pawback, triceps press, triceps pushdown, bench press, Yessis Machine sit-up, Russian twist, back raises with a twist and front arm raises.

Wednesday and Saturday
On Wednesday and Saturday, specialty work is done for specific skills and physical abilities. The exact work depends on your objectives and specific needs.

Most of you should be working on greater improvement of various soccer skills. Because of this it is important that you integrate the training so that you can include all of the different types of training in a timely and effective manner. As you do this specialized work, it gets closer and closer to actual competitive play. Thus by the end of this period of training you should be ready to begin competition.

PHASE THREE – THE COMPETITIVE PERIOD
During the competitive period your training should be devoted to maintaining the physical qualities already developed. You should not be increasing strength at this time because doing so will affect your technique. The key to the competitive period is in skill perfection and the ability to carry out the game skills in the various plays used by your team. You do not want increases in your physical abilities, except for speed and quickness in execution of soccer-specific actions. For example, a quick cut followed by a shot on goal or a quick sprint to reach the ball and execute a pass.

The main focus in the competitive period should be on perfection of technique and developing the psychological and strategic aspects of the game. These two aspects should be worked on together during the competitive period along with execution of the competitive game skills. You should do this in practice, in game scrimmages and in competitive game play. Keep in mind that your physical abilities should have been developed to their optimal levels during the specialized period of training.

Because the actual daily training workouts at this time depend to a great extent on your coach, no details are presented here. Suffice it to say that in practice you should be executing many plays and drills to enhance your play making ability as well as carrying out the strategies being developed. This is where your work on offense and defense becomes extremely important.

PHASE FOUR – THE POST-COMPETITIVE PERIOD

After competition you should go through a stage of recuperation and relaxation especially from a mental standpoint. At this time the body can still do physical work but the mind must rest. Active rest is best. This means that you remain active for relaxation purposes, not for physical development. At this time it is beneficial to participate in a different sport that you enjoy so that you can still experience the physical work but also get enjoyment and satisfaction from the playing to help you relax. The better your skills and abilities in this secondary sport, the greater will be your relaxation and enjoyment. The post-competitive period usually lasts from two to four weeks depending upon the length of your soccer season and how long it takes you to "wind down." This phase is very important and should not be omitted, especially if you play on a year-round basis.

However, if you hardly play during the season, then playing soccer in the post-competitive period can be very beneficial. It is at this time that you can put your game skills to work and to experience more competitive play. You do not have to relax at this time as does the girl who plays the entire game, every game. In addition, if you find that you are relatively weak and need greater strength you can immediately begin a strength training program. The more time you can spend developing strength then the more you will be able to develop speed and explosiveness to get you ready to play on a par with higher level players.

By using the schematic presented, it is possible to achieve the highest levels of speed and quickness, the keys to successful soccer play. Each period of training builds on the previous period of training and allows for the best performance during the competitive period. Equally important to ensuring that you get the most out of each training period, is the periodization of your nutrition. It is critical to eat and supplement your nutrition according to the training being done.

AVOID EARLY BURN OUT

If you go on a "crash course" to get in shape quickly (several weeks) you'll find it almost impossible to attain and to maintain top sports form for any appreciable length of time. This often happens to many players. Still others peak too early so that when major competition comes they are already burned out or begin to stagnate and can no longer perform at their best. These situations can easily be avoided.

Playing competitive soccer on a year-round basis is not the best way to become a better player. You must periodize your training. If you play constantly, especially in your youth, you may very easily burn out as you get into the teenage years. More effective is to get involved in other activities that can enhance your soccer playing abilities. Playing is very important, but mainly for development of strategy and the psychological qualities needed. Playing is not the best way to develop the skills of running, cutting and kicking. These should be worked on in separate trainings and then interwoven into the total game play as you mature over the years.

You must take each period of training in progression and let your body develop in a natural manner. Then when you peak you will be at your very best, capable of performing better than you have ever performed before. Equally important is that you will not experience the negative effects of overtraining and you will be able to start the next cycle of training fresh and healthy. This way you can again experience great gains for an even better season the following year.

CYCLING

Cycling means repeating the same action drill or exercise over a period of time, as for example, the leg action in running. In essence you repeat a certain number of repetitions for a few days, weeks or months. It also means repeating the same workout until you achieve a training effect, i.e., until you achieve the physiological changes in the body from the training that you do.

If you keep changing the training program every week, your body will not have a sufficient amount of time to attain the training effect. Keep in mind that the body adapts or increases in strength and other abilities only when there is repetition of a particular stimulus for a certain amount of time. The stimulus in this case is the exercise or workout that you are doing. You can keep adding additional resistance, but the exercises and number of sets and reps, should remain basically the same.

After your body adapts to the workout program a change is needed. You cannot keep repeating the same exercises or exercise routines over and over. The body will rebel in time from the boredom of the same routine and your muscle gains will cease and in some cases, show decreases.

When a particular exercise or exercise routine is repeated over too long a period of time, there is stagnation in the nervous system and the muscles are no longer stimulated to respond. This is a catch-22 situation. You must keep doing the exercises or exercise routine the same way for a certain period of time to get the maximum benefit from such a routine. Going beyond this time period brings about negative changes. Thus you must, at the right time, change the routine to get renewed energy of the nervous system and continued growth.

The key to success is in knowing when to make the necessary changes in order to restimulate the central nervous system. This is the secret to effective cycling which is possible only if you keep detailed diaries of your workouts. Most often you will see a leveling of results to signify full adaptation and an indication that a change is needed.

In general, high level, well conditioned and fit soccer players must change some basic exercises such as the squat every 4-5 weeks in order to see constant gains. Beginners and intermediates, however, may continue to experience gains for up to 3-4 months! Thus there is a wide gap between different levels of performers. When other exercises are looked at even greater variability can be seen. Because of this a differentiated approach is needed, and it must be geared to your level of fitness and exercise and sports mastery.

When cycling your workouts, you must not have many days of very intense workouts in a row. Most often you should have a hard day followed by an easy or a moderate intensity day and alternating in this manner over the week. When getting ready to peak (getting ready for competition), it is possible to have 2 or 3 heavy days in a row followed by some lighter days. Also after every 3 weeks or so – especially if the workouts are fairly intense – you should have a relatively light to moderate workout week to allow your body more time for full adaptation and to help the body recover, thus, preventing overtraining.

CONCLUSION

Many soccer players want a daily prescription in regard to what they should do for every workout. But as brought out above, this is impossible because each workout must be based on your abilities and only your abilities. Also the exact amount of time that you do each exercise or exercise program before changing the exercise or the workout routine depends upon your abilities.

Although the exact workouts for each of you cannot be presented, general guidelines on how the workouts should progress from the beginning of the year up to the time of competition are given. You have a great arsenal of exercises from which to choose and different types of training programs to bring about increases in strength, speed-strength, endurance, explosiveness, etc. It is simply a matter of selecting the exercises that will enhance your abilities the most and to incorporate them within the guidelines presented.

With sorrow many soccer training programs do not follow the guidelines presented mainly because the players do not train on a year-round basis or do not stay in shape on a year-round basis. Because of this general conditioning and getting ready for play often takes place in the pre-season, and the early games of the season are often used to continue preparing you for more intense playing. Some soccer programs even include heavy weight training at the beginning of the in-season. This should not be done as it interferes greatly with your running and cutting. All such work should be done well in advance of your playing.

By adhering to the recommendations presented in this book you will be able to not only play your best but become better in your soccer playing every year. Not only will your running and cutting be faster and cutting quicker, but you will be able to play the game at your best for the entire game.

Women's Issues

11

It is not uncommon to hear that women are different than men – aside from the obvious physical characteristics. For example, women are thought to be less athletic and considered to be the weaker sex. Women are considered to be slower than men, experience more injuries than men, and cannot generate the power needed for quick movements as can men. It is possible to go on with still other comparisons, but it would be fruitless, especially if you closely examine each of these beliefs. You will find that they are only partial truths that have been perpetuated over the years.

Significant differences in speed, power, and explosiveness do exist between men and women, but only at the extremes of the normal distribution of men and women. For example, the fastest men in the world are faster than the fastest women in the world. However, and this is most important to remember, the majority of men and women are basically equal in their speed capabilities. It is possible to find many women faster than men and vice-versa. In fact, women runners in recent Olympic games have broken men's speed records set in earlier years!

In regard to strength, the strongest men in the world are superior to the strongest women. This does not mean that all men are stronger than all women. There are many women who are stronger than men. If all other factors are considered equal, we would probably find as many men stronger than other men, as we can women stronger than other women, as we can the number of women stronger than men. Differences on the highest elite levels exist only between a relatively small percentage of athletes. About 90% of the females and males who participate in sports are more or less equally divided in relation to their strength, speed, power, coordination, flexibility, etc. In addition, the frequency and severity of injuries in soccer are lower than for men. And women are better at tolerating painful and other unpleasant sensations and strive more tenaciously to reach a goal that has been set.

I am sure that many of you can attest to this. I can recall having some young girls on teams that I coached surpassing the best boys in the league. But they were relatively few. Most girls and boys are fairly well balanced in the early years and because of this, it is possible to play boys with and against the girls. You should not keep thinking that all boys are superior to all girls when it comes to physical abilities or to playing soccer. Think in terms of equality. Only on the highest elite levels will you see a difference, and then the difference will only be with the outstanding players or teams.

More important to examine are some of the physical characteristics of women that should be taken into consideration in training. These differences appear to varying degrees in women and can effect your training and playing. Thus, it is important that you understand what they are and if they apply to you. Then you can take them into consideration in your training.

For example, a woman's physical work capacity is no more than about 80% of a man's. Because of this, adapting to physical loads involves considerable strain on the woman's body functions and produces a slower recovery. Women are also more excitable and react significantly more keenly to unfavorable situations. Even though women have less strength than men, women surpass men in precision, coordination and fluidity of movement when executing movements demanding these qualities. Women excel in long rhythmical work.

Flexibility

Most women have hypermobile joints (excessive flexibility), particularly at the elbow and knee joints. This should be taken into account in your weight training program as for example, when doing exercises such as the leg press and seated leg curl. If you relax the muscles when the legs are straight but under great tension, it can easily lead to injury Also the hypermobility in the knee joint can play a negative role in soccer play. To counteract the tendency to hyperextend the knee, it is important that you develop sufficient strength of the hamstrings (on the back of the thighs) to prevent the joint from going beyond its normal range of motion.

Knee joint hyperextension can occur in a stopping action when you plant the heel with a straight leg while your body is still moving forward. If your upper body forward momentum is great, there will be strong forces to hyperextend the knee, especially if it is already slightly hyperextended in the stopping action. Compounding the problem is that women have weaker ligaments, a greater amount of adipose tissue, and less muscle strength. Because of this you should also strengthen the quadriceps to not only stop your forward movement, but to help hold the knee in position. Use the muscles for the work to be done rather than relying on bone-to-bone pressure to do the stopping for you.

Skeleton

The female skeleton is generally smaller at the wrist, knees, shoulders, and ankle joints. Because of this, there is greater potential for injury in these joints. However, it is well known that the more one participates in a particular activity, the greater the adaptation of the body to withstand the stresses involved in that activity. For example, soccer players have stronger and thicker foot and ankle bones than non-players.

The finding that the female skeletal structure is generally smaller may be due to the activities in which women have typically been involved rather than a true, natural occurrence. For example, with training you can strengthen and increase the thickness and strength of the bones and ligaments to make the skeleton stronger and less prone to injury. The more stress you place on the bones, the stronger they will become.

Q Angle

Women have a greater Q-angle, the angle of the thigh bone in relation to the shin bone. The wider the hips the greater the angle of the femur and the greater the Q-angle, which increases the susceptibility to anterior cruciate ligament (ACL) damage. However, women who do exercises such as the squat, knee extension, knee curl, and straight leg hip adduction and abduction, rarely if ever experience ACL damage. Although surgeons note that women are generally more prone to ACL damage, I believe that most of the women who experience such damage are those who do not strength train most effectively to prevent such injuries.

Keep in mind that it is important to prepare yourself for the activity in which you will be involved. Soccer is a high-stress sport that requires many vigorous, dynamic movements. The forces experienced can be quite great. Therefore, you must physically prepare your body to be able to withstand these forces especially when playing all-out. The quick sprints, short stops, starts, tackling, etc., require great levels of fitness. You will not develop the optimal fitness levels needed merely by playing the game, you must do supplementary training to prepare the body for these stresses.

Force

Females generate muscular force slower than males in running and jumping. In other words, the reactiveness of the muscles is slower in women than it is in men. But, as with some of the other factors, this may be due to the minimal amounts and limited types of training that most women athletes have undertaken. For example, by doing explosive exercises, you can train the ability of the muscles to react faster and thus, generate more power. However, since women, as a rule, do not compete against men, this difference may be of little significance.

The key point to be remembered is that with proper training women can increase their speed of running and cutting. You can develop the ability to be more forceful and powerful in the movements involved. These are trainable characteristics but you must do the strength exercises to develop a firm base and then literally convert the strength into greater speed and power. Because most women have not done explosive training, which is the main method used for developing speed and quickness, many women do not see tremendous advances in their ability to make quick starts, dashes, and cuts.

Training

When you closely examine the major differences between men and women, it appears that many are due to cultural factors rather than innate physical factors. With more women participating in sport, these differences may become minimal over the years. But, and this is the most important factor, women must train to develop their abilities to the maximum. You must get more involved in strength training, not to be the strongest person on the team or to be stronger than the men, but to enable you to perform at your maximum potential.

In addition to the strength training, speed and explosive training is very important. These are areas in which women have typically not been involved. When you do become involved, especially with the exercises shown and described in this book, you will see dramatic changes in your playing ability.

Your strength and speed-strength qualities develop differently at different age periods. Most important are not increases in only strength, but increases in speed-strength, i.e., strength coupled together with speed. Such increases occur with the greatest intensity at ages 13 to 16.

It is important to understand that there is no correlation between your static strength and what you can display dynamically especially when coupled with speed. Many girls develop greater increases in strength, but if you do not work on developing greater speed-strength, the strength may not produce better overall play. This is especially true in the later teenage years if you have been strength training for some time.

With an increase in age there is improvement in the neuromuscular coordination in speed-strength type movements both in children and teenagers. This is still another reason why technique is so important in the early stages of training. The more you maximize and make your technique effective through neuromuscular coordination, the greater will be your display of speed-strength which equates to overall better soccer play. You will be able to execute the skills much more effectively, in addition to being faster and quicker in your movements.

Women who participate in sports more frequently and at a more intense level, show that the effects of such training are significant. Women who are physically better trained, have increased physical development more functional body reserves which allow them to do more, have greater resistive capacity and show improved adaptation to various unfavorable environmental influences. In addition, they have an easier course in pregnancy, childbirth, and post-natal periods and give birth to healthier children.

Endurance

The female functional potential expands significantly and approximates man's in a number of areas especially in endurance training. However, as the level of training increases, women athletes still do not achieve the adaptation that is peculiar to men or the level of development of the main physical qualities.

The potential for developing endurance is about equal in men and women, mainly because the circulatory and aerobic energy supply systems are trainable in identical ways. With regular training, a woman is able to achieve the same capacity for oxygen uptake with respect to body mass and her potential for using it is even greater. Thus, the female body shows excellent adaptability to endurance loads. Women do not experience more frequent damage to health than persons involved in other sports. However, soccer also demands great speed-strength to be successful. This is more difficult to attain.

Nutrition

Strength and explosive training play an extremely important role in becoming quicker and faster, but, for your training to produce maximum benefits, you must also have proper nutrition. This is an area in which many studies have shown time and time again that girls and women, more so than boys and men, have very poor diets that do not allow them to achieve their maximum potentials.

For example, one of the most common pitfalls that women and young girls fall into, is skipping meals in an effort to lose pounds. Doing this depresses your metabolic rate, and, as a result, you burn even fewer calories. As all studies show, eating more fiber, fruits, vegetables, complex carbohydrates, drinking at least 8-10, 8-ounce glasses of water daily, and not allowing yourself to get overly hungry, are still the best ways to maintain a balanced diet and not gain weight.

Women, more so than men, are more concerned with how their bodies look. This pursuit of the perfect body, especially when dictated by Hollywood or by certain celebrities, can have adverse long-term health consequences. Most troublesome is the common belief among women that thinner is better. This leads to three inter-related problems that women experience more so than men. This includes disordered eating, which covers a wide range of abnormal behavior which can be mild or even life-threatening. The other problems are amenorrhea, (delayed menarche) and osteoporosis (premature bone loss or inadequate bone formation).

In regard to disordered eating, women endurance athletes suffer from this problem much more so than men. Studies show that up to 70 or more percent skip meals or eat small meals in an effort to lose weight. Most often the women leave out many foods particularly those that contain fat. Because of the limitations placed on food choices, these women have diets that are nutritionally lacking not only in calories but in fats and other nutrients.

In regard to amenorrhea, there is typically an energy drain going on. The women do not take in sufficient calories to meet their energy expenditures. As a result, the brain decreases sex hormone production in response to the perceived starvation which results not only in the body retaining fat, but also causing amenorrhea. Such women are likely to have disordered eating habits more so than other women who have regular menstrual periods. In essence, the female body has evolved to where it can turn off its reproductive capabilities when there are extreme stresses which includes lack of food or what can be classified as famine, whether it be self-induced or environmental. As a result, these women have difficulty with conception or carrying a pregnancy to term.

When a woman has amenorrhea, and a deficient diet, there is decreased estrogen production which in turn places the women at a higher risk for stress fractures during training and premature osteoporosis. Keep in mind that peak bone mass is reached between the ages of 18 and 30. If the woman is amenorrheaic, she may be losing bone rather than gaining bone mass during the younger years which can lead to the early onset of osteoporosis. This is why it is so important to eat many green vegetables which are the main source of calcium for the body. Even though milk products are typically recommended, many studies show that the body does not absorb the calcium very well from these products, but does absorb the calcium very well from dark green vegetables. Calcium supplements as well as other supplements are not a replacement for a good healthy diet or to make up for an inadequate number of calories.

Another problem that women experience more often than men is iron-deficient anemia. This is especially important for soccer players, since iron, a major component of the red blood cells (hemoglobin) carries oxygen to the muscles and body tissues. Without ample iron, or more accurately hemoglobin, to get the oxygen to the working muscles and organs, you would be unable to perform well or for long periods.

The main reason many women experience iron-deficient anemia, is that they do not take in an adequate supply of iron-rich foods. Studies show that this occurs in approximately 75% of all women aged 18-44 and the numbers are substantial at even earlier ages. In addition, up to 50% of all female endurance athletes have depleted iron stores. Since endurance is one of the key components to playing well in soccer, it is something that you should be very cognizant of. When you begin feeling tired, it may be due to a lack of iron rather than other factors. However, by correcting your diet and eating a well-balanced diet with plenty of different foods, this problem can easily be taken care of as well as many other problems that seem to be common to women.

Note that the iron-deficient anemia problem is compounded because of the menstrual blood loss. Depending upon how heavy and how long the menstrual cycle lasts, it can account for a tremendous amount of iron loss. This is why some people recommend supplementing your diet with iron at this time, especially if you experience such losses.

Often overlooked with young girls who play soccer, is that their nutrition must provide for physical growth and development in addition to their playing. Having a poor diet in the preteen and teen years, will not only inhibit your playing but also normal growth patterns. Adults should not limit the amount of food that young girls eat in an effort to keep them thin. This may be worthwhile if the youngster is obese and inactive, but it certainly does not apply to youngsters who are very active, especially those involved in sports such as soccer.

Soccer is a very demanding sport that takes considerable amounts of energy. Thus, it is important that you eat ample amounts of food during the day to supply your soccer and growth needs. This is especially true of protein. There are no established limits for youngsters but some experts recommend over one gram per pound of body weight. Keep in mind that protein also provides some energy during play and is especially important for mental concentration.

Many people are guided by the recommended daily allowance (RDA) to determine how much nutritional intake they should have to meet their daily needs. For athletes, doing this can lead to poor growth patterns. The RDAs are based on a normal population which is typically sedentary. It does not apply to athletes, especially young athletes. Thus, I strongly recommend that you use the RDAs as bare minimums and, in many cases, double and even triple the amounts to make sure you get your nutritional needs met.

According to clinical nutritionist Dr. Tobin Watkinson, some females gain weight when they eat carbohydrates such as pastas, breads and potatoes. Most males, however, do not react this way. This may explain why some women often get sleepy after eating certain carbohydrates. The carbohydrates seem to react on the body the same way as protein does to other women. Because of this, it is important that you learn how your body reacts to the different nutrients and eat accordingly.

Although soccer players are mainly speed-strength athletes, there is also a strong endurance component. Because you have large training volumes, you may need twice or even three times as much energy intake (calories) per day as do athletes in track and field or gymnastics. However, there is a lack of documented data in regard to the energy that a child athlete expends when performing in a particular sport. Thus, it is important that you satisfy the nutritional demands of the body from the very earliest ages.

Another factor that must be taken into consideration is that the energy cost of activities such as walking and running is much higher in children than in adolescents and adults. The younger the child the higher is the cost of energy expenditure. For example, a 7-year old child could require as much as 30% more energy for every two pounds of body mass than a young adult when they both walk or run at the same speed.

The main reason for this is that much energy is wasted because of inadequate coordination of the muscles and the child's technique of walking and running. Most young girls have co-contraction of the muscles most of the time rather than having the ability to relax the muscle after it has performed its work. This is why working on technique of running, kicking, cutting, etc., is so important from the very earliest years. Instead of merely playing, young girls should learn how to execute the skills and then do more playing. At this time, the playing will then be much more effective and efficient in regard to energy expenditure, the key to playing long and hard.

The Menstrual Cycle and Reproduction

It has been shown quite convincingly that soccer and other sports have no negative effects on the reproductive system of a woman's body given a proper workout regime and training methodology. In fact, just the opposite has been found. Women athletes tolerate pregnancy and childbirth more easily and have sturdy, healthy children. Menstrual problems occur in women athletes of child bearing age no more often than in women who are not involved in a sport.

As a general rule, female athletes show a tendency for later onset of menstruation than other girls and show delayed sexual maturation. In some cases, there is even earlier maturation in female athletes. The difference appears to lie in the intensity and duration of the training.

Almost all studies done on women have found that the main reason for abnormalities in the reproductive functions among female athletes is excessive loads at the time when the sexual maturation develops. This is because the body's sensitivity to different stimuli at this time is especially high due to natural shifts in endocrine regulation and increased activity by hormones in the ovaries.

Researchers have noted that the more regularly young girls train, the easier their phase of puberty. However, they emphasized the dangers of maximal loads and of starting strict training sessions at this time. Many doctors believe that as the volume and intensity of the physical loads increase, so does the frequency of abnormalities. There is also a link between menstrual function problems and reduced body immunity.

Therefore, the pre-pubertal periods (especially ages 11-13) in a girl's life need particular attention from coaches and sports doctors. Most important is that extra care must be taken in the interval between the first menstrual (menarche) and the establishment of a stable menstrual cycle.

During properly designed training programs a new level of hormonal regulation gradually develops, one that provides for the body's adaptation to physical and neural stresses associated with the sports activity. If training is done without regard for changes in the female athletes condition in the menstrual cycle, the possibility that she will develop pathological changes in her ovaries increases.

In regard to menstruation and the ability of female athletes to perform, researchers have found that most women do not have to interrupt their training and participation in competition at the time of menstruation. Most of the women could perform at full strength, but, they also restrict their training during the period of menstruation. About 80% of female athletes achieve better results after menstruation and only about 3% do so during the pre-menstrual and menstrual periods.

Short-term intensive loads accelerate the onset of menstruation, but prolonged physical loads delay it. During menstruation, the female athlete's physical and mental state is different and adaptation to physical loads becomes more stressed and the recovery period is prolonged. The menstrual cycle has great significance on the work potential of women. The highest functional potential and work capacity shows up in the post-ovulatory period (days 16-24 of the cycle) and in the post-menstrual phases. The functional potential is lowest in the ovulatory phases (days 13-15 of the cycle). In this phase, circulation is least economical as is the use of the body's energy resources during physical loads. It is also the period of highest excitability. The higher the level of training, the less the negative phases of the menstrual cycle.

In the pre-menstrual phase, motor responses are worse and there are more frequent neural failures, a decrease in endurance, strength and speed of movements. In addition, there is a decrease in joint flexibility and increased tension of the joint ligaments.

Most doctors are in agreement that healthy female athletes with stable menstrual cycles and a good physical and mental state need no substantial change in their training regime during their menstrual periods. If there is deterioration in the physical and mental state, an unstable cycle, or a pronounced pre-menstrual syndrome, the total training load should be reduced, especially exercises for strength or speed and exercises that strain the body.

If there is pain, marked disturbance of various functions, and psychoneurotic reactions, the training load has to stop. A particularly sparing regime with complete exclusion of competition is needed at this time, and especially during sexual maturation.

Soccer Playing Development

The development of a soccer player can be divided into various stages, beginning with initial instruction up through the age of 12. The most effective instruction is between the ages of 10-12, since in the earlier ages you do not have sufficient strength and coordination to master the skills as needed. The development of the physical qualities such as strength, speed, quickness, etc., are most effectively developed between the ages of 12-18, especially if your technique is fairly good. Technique must be developed first after which you develop the physical abilities as they relate to your technique through the ages of 17-18.

Soccer requires a greater ability to develop short-lasting, maximum effort more than the ability to maintain it longer. Thus, speed-strength is more important than speed, cardiovascular endurance, or speed endurance. This is especially true of goalies, backs and forwards. The halfback position requires a higher endurance level than the other positions. Thus, the energy capacities of halfbacks are skewed more to the side of aerobic ability rather than anaerobic. However, both your anaerobic and aerobic capabilities must be fully developed. The higher their development the better you will be able to play and the more you can improve to play on higher levels.

SERVICES AVAILABLE FROM SPORTS TRAINING, INC.
- Biomechanical analysis of your running and cutting actions
- Analysis of your physical abilities
- A personalized exercise program
- Technique enhancement

Contact us for more information about any of the equipment used in this book.

Sports Training, Inc.
P. O. Box 460429
Escondido, CA 92046
Telephone: 877-DrYessis or (760) 480-0558
Fax: (760) 480-1277
Website: www.DrYessis.com
E-mail: dryessis@dryessis.com